43232001

Pretexts for *Writing*

Second Edition

Thomas Allbaugh
Azusa Pacific University

Kendall Hunt
publishing company

Cover image © Shutterstock, Inc.

Kendall Hunt
publishing company

www.kendallhunt.com
Send all inquiries to:
4050 Westmark Drive
Dubuque, IA 52004-1840

Copyright © 2009, 2013 by Thomas Allbaugh

ISBN 978-1-4652-2320-3

Printed in the United States of America
10 9 8 7 6 5 4 3 2 1

Contents

Chapter Three
Writing from Personal Experience   **47**

Chapter Four
Writing Arguments in Community   **75**

Chapter Five
Writing the Evaluation and Opinion Essay   113

Chapter Six
Inquiry, Invention, and Research   133

Chapter Seven
What We Talk about When We Talk about Style   165

Appendix
Title Writing Workshops   195

One of the most basic elements of a writing course is that we focus our students' attention on writing *as* writing. Writing itself becomes the subject of the writing course, which is typically structured in such a way that students are encouraged to develop, at least for a while, a hyperawareness of writing. It is a course in meta-writing. This intensified, and sometimes uncomfortable, awareness of writing as writing contributes substantially to an awareness of the experience of creativity itself. As beginnings, writing possesses the potential for making writers conscious of being on the threshold between doubting and believing, the personal and the public, the monological and the dialogical, conflict and accommodation, et cetera. This experience, in and for itself, defines the chief value of writing (142, 143).

Michael Carter

Where Writing Begins:

A Postmodern Reconstruction

Pre • **text** *n* 1 An ostensible or professed purpose; an excuse.

American Heritage Dictionary

Pretext and Acknowledgments

Donald Davidson calls them "prior theories" (qtd in Kent 4), those hunches we have about communication—about what we will say, how we will say it, and how we will be received. We bring these prior theories to writing, speaking in public, and even our conversations. I mean for the chapters here to address these prior theories. Here I call them "pretexts."

Another intention I had during the writing of this book concerned creating dialogues, in the best sense of that word. More than providing answers, I wanted to raise questions that might lead to dialogues, and then, possibly, to some answers. Each chapter starts with an argument about a particular topic of writing that usually passes as assumed. Usually—note chapter 2 as an example—the topic involves what many may have already learned about writing in earlier classes. Some topics—note chapter 4—are concerned with what we would probably call cultural assumptions about literacy. The way I think about it is this: As we learned to write in the past, we developed certain theories about writing, how writers write, and whether or not writing is even worth our time. This text addresses some of these preconceptions held by teachers and students, perhaps formed from previous lessons. *Pretexts for Writing* encourages dialogue about the ideas we often bring to writing, which is sometimes a task we do not fully understand.

*

By "pretext," I am referring to what happens before we write new text. The "pre-" stuff concerns what teacher and student bring to the tasks through past teachings and experiences.

To support this I begin with the assumption that the reader of this book has been in writing classes for a long time. The reader I have in mind may not have felt successful in these former classes. Though he or she may be taking a first college writing course, this reader has been writing for years, had writing classes, and has been graded on assignments. Though there certainly are many more strategies this reader needs to learn, both for college courses and later for the profession she or he plans to enter after graduation, this reader is not in this class as a blank slate. He or she is certainly not without anticipation about the tasks that lie ahead in class. Quite probably he or she has already formed opinions about succeeding in the course, and even whether it is worthwhile to learn to write for new audiences. Perhaps underneath this uncertainty is the certain knowledge that writing, after all, is an arduous task. To do it well, we need more than mere inspiration or passion for our subject. We need more than a few simple rules like "Never use the first person pronoun 'I'" or "Never begin a sentence with 'because'." We face new intellectual tasks; we need to learn strategies.

This book, then, takes writing as its subject. And it is important to resist two strong tendencies right from the start: The first is a reaction, this idea that we've heard it all before, so it's not worth our time. The second is the tendency to think that it's all new. Indeed, perhaps much of what is in this textbook is a rerun, but it is a rerun in a new set of circumstances and following from slightly different pretexts than before. As I say in one of the chapters to follow, learning to write is never like learning math equations. The reason is simply because with writing in college for the first time, writers find themselves speaking to new, more sophisticated audiences than they did in high school. The math equations may be the same ones they worked out in high school algebra; but that high school five-paragraph theme and rules about first person pronoun "I" are so basic that they won't take anyone very far with college readers.

Each chapter takes a position on the subject it examines. Each addresses some of the most common assumptions that people hold and suggests better ways to think about and practice writing. To facilitate this approach, each chapter begins with a featured prompt, and response is invited. Between chapters, grammar interludes provide guidance on points of prescriptive grammar that can lead to understanding the most commonly used punctuation patterns. These interludes can be treated as homework and then addressed in ten minutes or so at the beginning or end of class, or even brought in at the beginning of peer sessions with rough drafts. They are meant to remind readers of what is not that hard to know about nouns, verbs, modifiers, phrases, and clauses. If a class spends a few minutes on each of these every week, students can build a writer's knowledge of these categories so that they can examine their own sentences as most writers do. These lessons culminate in and coincide with the final chapter on style. Building on these grammar interludes will prepare students to have the proper background to think productively about what an effective writing style is.

As is probably obvious, discussion of organization in terms of "modes," which are presented in most textbooks as stable patterns, has been downplayed. In place of the modes, organization is chiefly figured here in terms of genres, which are not stable, but certainly more in line with writing in the professions. The preferred focus on report writing, argumentation and evaluation, and research argumentation here is meant to be an introduction, and this can be built on in later courses in writing in the disciplines.

Finally, I assert many times in the following pages that writing sometimes seems like a solitary activity, but it is never done alone. From our teachers to our colleagues, our peers, and even our enemies, we have many collaborators who help us to do better work than we would have done without them. This is also true of this book, and I would like to acknowledge those who helped to make this work possible. I am grateful to Azusa Pacific University for the opportunity I had to take a sabbatical for the spring term of 2008, during which all of the first draft of this book was composed. I am grateful to Dr Michael Whyte, provost at Azusa Pacific University, who encouraged me in the sabbatical during which most of this book was written, and who also continues to support the Freshman Writing Seminar program at APU. I am grateful to Dr David Weeks, Dean of CLAS at Azusa Pacific University, for his support of my sabbatical and for his ongoing interest in many of the concerns raised in this book. Thanks are due to Dr David Esselstrom, my department chair, for first signing off on my sabbatical project, and for ongoing discussions of rhetoric, especially the importance of imagination in writing for audiences.

I would also like to thank my editors, Lacey Reynolds, Amanda Smith and Shelley Walia at Kendall Hunt, for their help in the process of publication.

I am also indebted to the following colleagues and friends for their direct influence on the writing of this book, as well as their support.

To the Ninos of Southern California, an artists' prayer group, for ongoing support and encouragement;

Thanks to my wife, Bernadette, for her ongoing love and support, for reminding me not to over-revise, and for those sabbatical lunches I looked forward to having with her simply because we could have them.

To Rachel, Carolyn, Matthew, and Michael, my daughters and sons, I owe a debt of gratitude for their tireless acceptance of their dad as distracted by writing and sometimes bringing up random concerns at the dinner table, but also for being so much fun to be around.

Finally, I dedicate this book to the memory of my father, Floyd Allbaugh, a journalist of the old school, who gave me my first real writing lessons with the words, "good writing results from rewriting." I see this book also as part of his legacy.

Work Cited

Kent, Thomas, ed. Introduction. *Post-Process Theory: Beyond the Writing-Process Paradigm.* Carbondale and Edwardsville: SIU Press, 1999.

Chapter One

What Matters about Writing Processes

Chapter Overview

This chapter introduces two ideas: Writing is a subject worthy of your study; and the first order of that study has to do with invention. This chapter centers on a cognitive approach to invention by looking at the differences in the way that two different musical composers created their work. Comparisons between writing music and writing different kinds of essays suggest specific ways to think about different intellectual tasks in different writing assignments. A final concern features suggestions and strategies for getting started on the writing assignments required in college.

First Thoughts

Does writing come easily only to the gifted? Or is it also a subject that should be studied? These questions get at deeply ingrained attitudes. If writing is a subject worthy of study, then what should be done in a writing class? The narrative following Writing Prompt 1 on the next page suggests more about what should not be done. But even in this, the negative answer is still a beginning—if writing is something that can be learned.

feature 1.1   Writing Prompt 1

Thinking through Analogies

An analogy builds a comparison between two different things, one usually abstract or undefined and the other concrete and familiar. The comparison is made to make the abstract knowable. "Shall I compare thee to a summer's day?" asks Shakespeare of his lover. Many poets and popular singers have compared love (abstraction) to a rose (concrete, familiar), even a sick rose. Analogy, also known as simile, strikes the comparison by using the words "as" or "like": "Driving the new car Model XXX (unknown) is like riding on a magic carpet (more familiar)," an advertiser might croon. In contrast, the writer for *Consumer Reports* may find the new car Model XXX to "ride like an old stagecoach, with plush, luxurious seats that do not protect the rider from all the bumps of the road the driver will feel because of the poor suspension system."

Analogies can be longer than a single line. Some writers create analogies that become sustained over many points of comparison. "Here," they will note, "are the ways in which the new economic crisis (abstract) is like a tsunami (concrete) for most tax payers." The comparison between economic disaster and natural disaster is exploited for powerful effect that develops several points.

To get started in thinking about the ideas presented in this chapter, engage in the art practiced in many academic majors: the art of comparison, or sustained analogy. Think about something you like to do that requires your involvement and practice in tennis, swimming, reading about history, or painting. Can it be used in a comparison to writing? How far can the comparison be sustained before it breaks down?

Begin your response to this prompt with the words "Writing is like..." or "Writing can be compared to...." Or perhaps, if it fits, begin with, "Writing, shall I compare thee to a summer's day (or to your more deeply personal passion)?"

Following this, develop several points of comparison or points that show how writing and your chosen passion cannot be compared. Develop this in several paragraphs. Explain your past experiences with writing, doing so in terms familiar to you and to your audience. After writing, reflect on what your comparison suggests about how you might best approach continuing to learn to write.

Also, consider extending the idea of analogy and metaphor. How much of the way we communicate through language includes the use of these tropes?

"You Will Write a Paper That Has a Thesis . . ."

Listen. Here's what happened in my first college writing course.

English 101, Fall, 1974. Our teacher, still young, wore leisure suits, usually brown or green. His hair covered his ears and his collar, and curled over the dark frame of his glasses. This is to say that he fit right in.

Early on, during the first week of the semester, he told the story of Plato's "Allegory of the Cave." He drew a chalk fire, stick figures, and a wall on the board to assist him in his telling.

The allegory went like this. Men were chained in a cave from birth and required to look straight ahead at shadows dancing on the wall in front of them. They couldn't even see each other, only the shadows. One of these men was suddenly unchained and forced to look around him at the real men chained next to him and at the fire and the figures behind him. And then (this was a slow process) he was brought out of the cave and into the light of day, where he saw for the first time real trees, the sun, other people, and not just shadows of them. After seeing all of this and then beginning to enjoy this truer life than the one he'd known in the cave, he formulated a moral decision he would have to make. He could go on in the light, enjoying his new understanding of himself and the world around him, or he could take this new understanding and return to the cave to tell the others about where they really were. What would he do now?

Plato's answer for this newly enlightened individual was given in the dialogue. Go back. Tell them. In terms eerily similar to the fate of his own teacher, Socrates, this newly freed man returned to the cave and was killed by those still chained there. They didn't want to hear about what he had seen.

I knew this story had something to do with what Plato believed were the purposes of education. It seemed to be saying that education has more to it than identifying a career path or providing job training. Education has something to do with enlightenment, with moving from a happy ignorance to the painfully bright lights of being informed and no longer bound by prejudices. For those men coming out of the cave, enlightenment would be painful.

This was Plato's allegory of the cave. It made learning seem precarious, even dangerous. Weighty issues seemed to loom before me. But after the class period in which we discussed it, the professor went on to other matters, and from then on, nothing in the class built on Plato's allegory. I suppose the story was concerned in a general sense with what I was experiencing as a new college student. But what it had to do with writing was not clear.

Next, we were assigned a research paper, our main project for the semester. Along with this, a few small assignments came up. For example, early on I submitted a handwritten paragraph or two on how all of life is about change. Writing it out in pen was acceptable in this time before personal computers, though the research paper, we were told, would have to be typed. I had already written many research papers. Most of the time—for government class, for history, or for English—I could choose my own topic. In 12th-grade English, I had been required to go through many formal steps to writing a research paper. So this college paper was more of the same, except that I remember the professor required that the paper have a thesis. It was, as I recall, his main requirement. He did not expect us to hand in index cards with sources and notes on them. He did not ask for an outline before we wrote the paper. These had both been required by my 12th-grade teacher. She had required an outline written in complete sentences with Roman numerals and the usual rules that applied to outlines (if you have an A, then you must have a B; if you have a 1. you must have a 2). I wasn't prepared to question why I should have a 2 if my subject or my thinking did not have one. But now my professor only required a final paper that was thesis driven. And he did expect an outline to serve as a kind of table of contents, or perhaps an outline, showing the shape of my paper. I do not remember him ever lecturing us on documentation method—all of that seemed to be taken as assumed on our part, the stuff we had mastered in high school.

Days before the deadline, I checked books out of the library on the German reformer Martin Luther. As I began to write, the sole requirement (beyond the assumption that I would document my sources) came to me, and as I read and wrote, I began to think about my focus. The main requirement did not stop me from writing the paper in my own way, as a biography; it just had me thinking about how to bend what I was writing to meet the requirement. This finally came to me in the last few paragraphs: Martin Luther should be held up as an example of what happens when individuals stay true to their convictions. This was my thesis, stated at the end of the paper, where I argued that his whole life was an emblem of this.

I wrote this draft on a Smith Corona typewriter. I completed the reference page, which I titled "Bibliography."

A few weeks later, my professor's remarks on my paper were memorable. He wrote that some of the paper was well written (I assumed that he was referring to what I had written, and not to my sources), but that the whole thing amounted to "setting up a cannon to kill a mosquito." He had captured what was wrong with my thinking.

Today I sometimes wonder, though, what might have come of that experience if I had been required to meet with him to discuss how to revise the paper. Or what if I had been allowed intervention on his part early on, before I chose my topic, so that he could have steered me into a better topic or, perhaps, a better way of approaching the topic I had? What if he had demonstrated thesis statements that did work appropriately, that didn't result in scribal nuclear winters? What if we'd spent some time on this one major requirement for the paper?

As it stood, I had written a narrative and then made up a poorly considered main idea at the end of it. When I think today about that last-ditch "main idea," I realize that I was guilty of doing a "make-over," of turning Martin Luther, a deeply religious man from the late middle ages, into an example of a late twentieth-century individualist.

If I had been able to talk with my teacher about all of this, what would have happened? What would I have learned, about history, about ideas, about my own deeply ingrained assumptions regarding community and individualism? What would I have learned about writing as the subject of the course?

Assume That Writing Is a Subject We Should Study . . .

My first writing class in college was conducted in the old style. The teacher gave an assignment and then required a final draft. I suspect he probably assumed that we should have already learned in high school how to go about completing the assignment. Yet as I think I demonstrated, I didn't really know how I was supposed to write a thesis statement.

This was a class I took decades ago. But it is similar to the way that many college professors today still handle the writing assignments they give. To them, writing is not really a subject but a set of rules for format, organization, and style. Or they think of it as a subject they can't teach. Or perhaps many teachers in the courses you will take in your major and in other electives over the next four years will assume that you already have learned how to write the papers they will assign. They will give the assignment and then, after a period of time, collect the final drafts. The possibility that their writing assignments are really tasks you have never tried before will not occur to them.

This doesn't mean that they are right. Most of the research on writing published since the 1970s has concerned what writers do at different stages of development. Many composition researchers have been interested in how students new to college must learn to handle their most challenging new intellectual tasks. Most obviously, researchers have found that to be effective, writers engage in some sort of process. That process, as the next section shows, may vary from assignment to assignment. For longer, more complex writing never tried before, the writer may start with initial ideas and then shape and reshape them through several stages of invention and then a series of drafts. Successful writers in business, education, politics, and the sciences—not just in English—work this way.

But there is also the concern for college students to get practice in these new genres of writing they are being assigned, which may mean being given more than one chance to write a certain kind of paper that a professor knows is important to his or her discipline. Process and certain kinds of focused, guided practice allow writers to learn to write well for new audiences.

Certainly, when it comes to process, many students and teachers who don't write very often will take a "one size fits all" approach to writing assignments, taking the same approach to a long research paper that they would to a short essay, especially if they don't care about the assignment. I think I demonstrated that in my first year writing class I probably took the wrong approach to both kinds of writing I did. When I wrote my little piece about life as a place where only change was constant, I actually wrote three or four different versions. It was small enough, and it mattered enough to me, that I tried different wordings and even altered the order of the two paragraphs, trying out the best way to say it. Today I think that my topic was trite. But I did more to rework this piece than I did with the research paper. For some reason I can't really fathom now, I was more invested in writing expressively at the time.

We might consider these ideas about writing processes more productively if we draw on illustrations from other fields.

Writing as Making a Free Throw or Hitting a Baseball

Ever watch basketball players shoot free throws? These are the shots they are given with no one blocking them. They simply stand ten feet from the basket, take their time while everyone watches them, and shoot the ball. One would think that a professional, paid millions of dollars, could make these shots with eyes closed. But that is the subject for another setting. For the present, note that when basketball players do go to the free throw line, they will sometimes perform a ritual before they shoot. They will dribble the ball twice, slouch once, blink, and then shoot. Or they will dribble the ball once with the right hand and once with the left hand. Then they will shoot.

Do they think that if they don't do this ritual first they will miss?

Many baseball hitters are like free throw shooters. They perform a ritual before they try to settle in and take a swing at a 95-mph fast ball coming at them. They need to concentrate, and what they do before they step in is meant to sharpen that concentration. Some hitters give the sign of the cross; some shake their shoulders and touch their noses. Some spit out chewing tobacco and blink twice.

Only twice.

It helps them concentrate.

One teacher of writing has noted that writers sometimes do certain rituals when they sit down to write that bring to mind the way that some free throw shooters step up to the free throw line or baseball batters settle into the batter's box before each pitch. They do this because it helps them concentrate. Writing requires as much concentration as these other activities.

Rotten Apples, Cigarettes, Mozart, and Beethoven

American poet Stephen Spender has observed that writing poetry requires concentration (48). But he also notes that different poets and writers attain this level of concentration on their work in different ways. Schiller, he writes, kept rotten apples under his desk because the smell allowed him to think deeply. Walter de la Mare smoked to get focused, a habit that Spender shared. In fact, his smoking habit was mostly centered around his writing. Spender also categorizes poets in terms of their relationship to their own unconscious minds. He suggests that some poets enjoy a close connection to their unconscious and compose pieces that require little to no revision. But there are also those, Spender suggests, who must "write their poems by stages, feeling their way from rough draft to rough draft, until finally, after

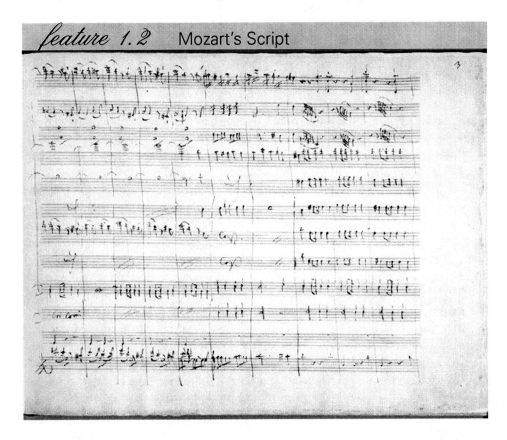

Feature 1.2   Mozart's Script

feature 1.3   Beethoven's Script

many revisions, they have produced a result which may seem to have very little connection with their early sketches" (48).

Spender sees these two different processes demonstrated in the work of composers Wolfgang Amadeus Mozart and Ludwig van Beethoven. Mozart, the subject of the 1980s film *Amadeus,* is of the first type. He wrote quickly, and Spender describes him as having worked out "whole symphonies, quartets, even scenes from operas, entirely in his head—often on a journey or perhaps while dealing with pressing problems" (48). In a comical scene from the movie *Amadeus,* Mozart is shown turning a shouting tirade from his mother-in-law into an aria for one of his operas. It would appear that his ideas came to him fully developed, and all he had to do was write them down. Mozart, Spender would argue, lived very close to his unconscious mind.

In contrast, Beethoven worked slowly from life, taking years to plan and write a single work. His manuscripts show evidence of labor, with much crossing out and much revision going on. By most accounts, he went for long walks with little more than themes in his head and had to reflect for long periods. Spender notes that Beethoven worked haltingly, and he kept ideas in notebooks for years, letting them take root and incubate (48).

Most writers, composition scholars have suggested, can resemble either Mozart or Beethoven. Janet Emig, in writing of the use of the unconscious, draws on Spender's illustration of Beethoven and Mozart when she writes that "the Mozartian is one who can instantaneously arrange encounters with his unconscious" (52). In contrast, she notes, the "Beethovian is the agonizer . . . a plodding miner who seems to scoop south with his bare hands" (52). Emig makes the important connection to writing. When teachers give classroom assignments that are themes assigned with no call for rough drafts, she points out, they act as though anyone who can write should be like Mozart (52).

But not every writer can tap deeply into the subconscious mind for fully developed ideas on demand. Not even Beethoven could do this. But this does not mean they are not writers. In fact, it may be more realistic to say, when talking about writing for school, that, as writers, we can resemble either of these composers at different times. After all, Mozart, who seemed to experience his work as whole visions, was writing in forms that had become predictable. His symphonies, for example, followed a pattern already worked out. Beethoven, who was breaking new ground in terms of this same form, worked haltingly, slowly, playing back to himself what he'd already written, working out new plans and new puzzles.

A brief consideration of the sonata form will be helpful for this point. When Beethoven began his career, the pattern of organization for first movements of symphonies was called sonata form, a musical pattern so clearly defined that it had built up audience expectations akin to the Hollywood happy ending or the three-act movie structure. Those expectations had been defined by the classical form developed by Franz Joseph Haydn.

In Haydn's formation, sonata form followed a three-part pattern. Audiences listened for it, and part of their listening pleasure had to do with recognizing the form itself. The first part of the sonata form consisted of a section called the exposition, in which the main themes of the movement were stated. These themes would be presented in a pleasing order, and this order might be repeated. Then, in the second part of sonata form, called the development section, the themes announced in the exposition would be given variations, stated in fragmented ways, rendered in another key, and generally developed. This middle section, which would cast all of the themes in a new light, would then give way to a third section, called recapitulation, which would return to the original key of the movement and replay all of the themes announced earlier in their rediscovered, full form.

The third section, especially in the symphonies of Haydn and Mozart, usually sounds triumphant, sometimes dramatic and convincing, but it is always announced obviously by the full statement of the first theme of the exposition. It is as though the opening of the symphony were being given again. The last six symphonies of Mozart are perhaps supreme examples of this classical form.

Both Haydn and Mozart followed the form with only one variation: In a few of their symphonies, they began with a slow section, a sort of prologue, that led up to the announcement of the first exposition, or thematic section.

When Beethoven came on the scene as a young composer, Mozart and Haydn were both writing their most mature music. Beethoven studied briefly with Haydn and, of course, came of age in the wake of many changes happening to the political structures around Europe, including the French Revolution. Still, his first symphonies sound much like those of his teachers. However, Beethoven was up to something new in his third symphony, where he followed the usual form noted above for the first two sections of his first movement. But when he came to the recapitulation, where Mozart or Haydn would return to a full, triumphant announcement of the first theme, Beethoven skipped this and simply entered the recapitulation without announcement or fanfare, skipping to the second, tentative exploration of the first theme.

Of interest is that Beethoven was playing not just with a musical form but also with his audience's expectations. And he didn't do it right away. He waited a few years until he'd had some initial successes with the conventional ideas and demonstrated to everyone that he wasn't making mistakes out of incompetence before he made his experiments public. But it is pretty easy to see this: With the experiments he was conducting with sonata form, it took him a longer time to fully work out these new variations on the old form than if he had simply followed the old pattern.

Mozart and Beethoven on the Research Essay

When you get a writing assignment, what do you do? Do you write it the night before it is due?

Consider this. We may not only be defined as writers in terms of being a Mozartian—someone who writes quickly from a whole understanding of our writing intentions—or a Beethovian, someone who must work in fits and starts; we also might take our cue from these two composers by understanding that different intellectual tasks will have us working now like a Mozartian, now like a Beethovian. Everything will depend upon the intellectual task we have been assigned. If the assignment is short, not complex, or one we've seen before and fully understand, like telling a story of something that happened to us or writing a five-paragraph theme or a comparison-contrast essay, we might be able to work fairly quickly. But this probably won't be true if the assignment is new to us; if we are being asked to write ten or twenty pages based on researching a subject new to us, a subject we have many questions about, we may, like Beethoven, need more time in which to work out all of our problems with the new subject and form.

This is an important consideration. Most assignments in college will be new. They will require new intellectual responses. In many ways, you are like Beethoven, playing with new developments, not Mozart. Since this is the case, the question to ask next concerns this: What practical things can help to write effectively for these new tasks? What strategies for inventing, drafting, revising, and editing might help?

But Real Writers Don't Do That. They're Like Mozart.

At first blush, the discussion of the two composers above would seem to focus only on the literal act of writing music—or words—down on paper. What is really underscored in their accounts, as Spender and Emig have noted, more deeply concerns how creative people relate to their unconscious mind in their creative work. Writing, as a creative activity and as a form of communication, is not easily reduced to merely following a few simple rules and then putting words on paper. If you have studied writing as nothing more than following a short set of rules—"Never use the first person pronoun 'I'," "Never use contractions," "Always begin your essay with a generalization," "Begin every paragraph with a topic sentence," and "Every paragraph should have seven sentences"—then you

feature 1.4   The Thinker

© aquatic creature, 2009. Used under license from Shutterstock, Inc.

should question whether these rules are actually preventing you from writing well. Like most endeavors that involve being human, writing can and does involve different processes.

Some, of course, will object to this. This is not what the real writers do, they will say. But do we know what "real" writers do? Or is this another of our assumptions about creativity? What goes into the makeup of a "real" writer, as with discussions of what makes a "real man" or "woman," has been steeped in stereotype and contradiction. As with the assumptions of the men chained in Plato's allegory, we may have had little real experience with the subject. Before we get very far in life, what we believe about "real men" will color our behavior, our attitudes, even our life goals. Some of these stereotypes are conventional. The trouble with our beliefs about what real writers do is that we have been taught them by people in authority, and these are difficult to unlearn. What we believe about writers and writing will determine how we approach writing. If we reduce writing to a series of rules, these rules may actually get in the way of our generating effective prose. Perhaps we can underscore a few important issues about writers—real writers are not necessarily published novelists, poets, or short story writers. Real writers write for any number of purposes. And real writers are in great demand in business departments, psychology departments, and the sciences.

Of course, not all students or teachers want to learn to write or think that writing is as important as the subject they most care about—economics, sociology, theology, history, or biology. The opposite of this, however, is equally valid: Wonderful writers and teachers of writing can be found in every discipline in college, not just in English departments.

A List of Strategies

Inventing our ideas—first coming up with ideas that seem workable, and then developing those ideas for certain forms and audiences—may have been the part of writing that was either ignored in your previous classes or reduced to a few simple rules. But what real writers do at this early stage most resembles either children at play or television script writers closeted away in a room with pizza and plenty of coffee. Or, as already noted, this stage can resemble a rigid, fixed, boxed-in approach in which the writer simply works in patterns she has used before, defaulting to a basic form and not considering audience. But if allowed, there can be an element to this process that is creative, and it is this aspect of writing that is not a part of what most of us were taught to do.

People who write on the job have noticed that the more they write, the better they get at it. They may not always need to spend time on invention strategies. But when they do have a complicated writing project to accomplish or one they haven't done before, they may, like Beethoven, have trouble concentrating on the task. They have learned to think about writing as a form of problem solving. So to get their mind on task, they jot down notes to themselves. This might be an outline of what needs to be done, or it may involve thinking through what they already know about the project. This will help them to think about what they still need to learn. They might start by using certain strategies that force them to put words on paper. For them, inventing starts with activities—brainstorming, freewriting, talking to friends or relatives, or outlining are typical. A useful strategy for many writers involves keeping a notebook. What I like about a notebook is that it is a place to write in every day when the writing doesn't have to be formal.

More recent elaborations on the invention theme might include cubing (looking at a topic from six different angles), Burke's dramatistic pentad, and the act of clustering. Each of these would be good to try out depending on what your immediate problem is. What I like about all of them is that they are not final products. I will not be graded or judged for them. If they don't work, I drop them. The main point is not the activities themselves but the way that they get me on track with certain ideas that I can follow up on.

There are also other ways to think about invention. Consider that invention could also be served partly by social means—as helping us to explore different possibilities open to a subject. Through conversations with others, especially others who may think differently than we do on a topic, we can begin to think in fresh ways before writing about a subject. In this, you might consider that on choosing your subject you will want to entertain three or four different ways of thinking about it: How would these differing perspectives make your subject look? For example, if I were to consider my story above about my first research paper in college, how would that look if I considered the teacher's perspective as well as my own? Writing from a different, imagined perspective can lead to new insights, ideas, and content.

Whatever we decide to do, consider that the activities listed here—brainstorming, freewriting, outlining—are all meant to serve an initial exploration of a new topic. Clearly, considered this way, just having passion for your subject may not take you as far as you think it will. Usually, if we do not move through a time of invention first, our rough draft—which will be all over the place anyway—will certainly be more like invention than a finished draft. In fact, because the first draft that most writers compose will show a lot of new discoveries being made in the act of writing, the dividing line between invention as a stage and drafting may actually be more accurately rendered as a dotted line or even a half step on a continuum. The truth is that though we often have moved to composing our thoughts for an audience and in a given form in our first draft, our first draft will look like a very young child. It will still have a lot of baby fat. It will still show those signs of invention and discovery going on in it.

Pretext: On Invention
Some Ways to Think about Beginning

As should be clear from some ideas in this chapter, writers, like baseball players and philosophers, need warm ups. But they also enter into writing with a mixture of experiences and vague, unrealized notions. They begin by opening up their minds and bringing out this strange mixture and making sense of it. Usually this is done using some method of discovering what they have to say about their subject. For some projects, drafting is the way into discovery, and this will mean revising.

The following strategies can be warm ups; they also offer methods of discovery. Remember that the following provides for a discussion of strategies, not a stage of writing to leave behind. If composition scholars are to be believed, then you might find yourself returning to this chapter, perhaps even this section of this chapter, again and again, even after you have written a second draft of a paper. Without any reference to new technology or gimmick, we might think of this textbook as a circular one, "recursive," as many composition scholars note. Try several of these methods with each paper you work on.

I've used all of these methods, and some of them once helped me more, when I was still developing, than they do at present, when I'm still developing in new ways. Others I use. I'm looking for a way to begin my writing that will result in a successful performance. But in invention, what needs to happen is this: I need to discover my subject matter and my focus on it (this usually amounts to a thesis), as well as the organization I will use (comparison-contrast? argument? narrative with flashback?), the style or voice I will tell it in, and perhaps most important (sort of in a last but not least way), who my audience is. None of the following does it all. And I'm not mechanical about this. The main point behind why writers invent is not to have a draft done but to do enough thinking and gathering of ideas so that they can write a draft. Try combinations. But your assignment, if your teacher agrees, is to choose at least one of these—preferably two or more—to do for the rest of the semester. Between you and your teacher, decide on how you will experiment with these suggestions and how you will be graded. Plan to write some concluding thoughts after you have experimented with two or more of them for the term.

Freewriting

This method was popularized by a group of compositionists and writers known as "expressionists." This method especially helps when you face writer's block. It is also a valuable way to learn to write more fluently, especially if you stop after every sentence you write to change it, reword it, correct it. Twenty-five years ago, I did a great deal of freewriting, and it helped me to begin writing fluently. In fact, many chunks of thought, or paragraphs in this section, were the results of freewrites. I've revised them, of course, but the main idea, the main substance, and in many cases, the best words and phrases, came from a freewrite.

To do a freewrite, write nonstop for a certain length of time. Do not rush. Simply write without stopping to check on what you've written. Like journaling, freewriting can help to develop confidence in writing, it can help with developing sentences, and it can help with developing ideas. What I like about freewriting is that after I've done it, I actually have words on the page to work with. I'm no longer staring at an empty page wondering where to begin. To freewrite, choose a topic and focus it, or simply write to find out what is in your head. But the minute you stop to check on your wording, you are no longer freewriting. You have stopped. Don't do this, even if you run out of things to say. If that happens, simply write, "I can't think of a thing to say, I can't think ..." until a new thought appears and leads you on. Only stop when the timer does or when you have enough.

Writing a Letter to a Famous Dead Person or to a Family Member or Close Friend

This method can work like freewriting. It can free up your style a little. It can get you comfortable with your subject, and it gets you thinking a little bit about writing for an audience that is not threatening (unless your famous dead person, or your cousin or your aunt, is a famous writer). Simply compose an informal letter in which you tell your correspondent about your subject, what's at stake in it, the consequences of it, what your correspondent may think of it, and what it may lead to or have started from. Sign your letter. Don't send it, though, as this is really writing to yourself. On second thought, perhaps you could send it, as it might lead to a dialogue if your person is still alive. You might learn new information that you can use to change your thoughts, add to them, or modify them. If you do send it, certainly make a photocopy of it for your own use.

Keep a Journal

This is not like the proverbial diary in which you tell the page about your dating life. This is like a lab. I use a journal to write various kinds of passages. Sometimes I jot down a phrase or idea that has come to me for the first time, either because I like the catchy way it is worded, or because I want to develop it more later. Sometimes, after thinking for a while, I'll sit down and in my journal try to capture my thinking about it as fully and formally as I can. Sometimes, I will write down conversations because they capture the way people talk, the way language works, or they capture an experience I might actually use in a story or to support an idea. Other times, I'll write down a passage I've read because it is well written, I like the style, or I want to save the important idea. Sometimes my journals are focused on a topic, like a notebook I'm keeping for one project. Sometimes they are random and all over the place. The thing that I find more enjoyable about writing in a journal is that it is private, but it is private in the way that a child's play area is private. The child, in this area, can try on new roles, new experiences. She can play at being married, at being a priest, at being a teacher, lining up her dolls in front of her and writing on a blackboard. In the same way, I can, in the privacy of my journal, pretend to be an expert on a subject and begin writing about it. I can discover that the style is pompous and give it up, or I can go with it and play until I discover the proper style. But no one has to see this play, and it certainly won't be graded. I like this private-public play area that a journal can become. Some researchers have suggested that journal writing can lead to greater fluency and confidence in writing. I've found that it has helped me in these areas.

List Making

Before writing, some writers like to put down on paper, as a kind of roadmap or suggestion of the possibilities, one or more lists of things that they will go into. These lists consist of little more than "notes to self," the sort of thing that we want to remember. It's exciting when the list making has its own generative quality and suddenly takes on a life of its own, and we see new connections and where we want to start and what we want to say. This doesn't always happen. I usually list items before I start writing so that I can remember them, but also, more importantly, because the list can serve as an initial, tentative organization principle that my first drafting can follow (I'll often change this organization later).

Keeping a Notebook

This can take several forms. It can just be random notes scribbled on everything from a napkin in a restaurant or scrap paper next to your bed, to an actual notebook in which you jot down how your essay or project is developing. You write down examples as they come to you, things people have said about your subject, new ideas, generalizations, possible beginnings, and sentences that seem to express the ideas for you. This captures the idea that we are writers not only when we are sitting at our desk and writing. We often get our ideas while driving to the grocery store, when we are sitting in a sports bar, or when we wake up in the middle of the night. One of my teachers gave as her definition of a writer the following: "A writer is not necessarily someone who has published. A writer is someone who can be seen jotting down ideas for an essay or a story while they are at the zoo with their preschooler. Anyone taking down notes for a larger project when they are away from the desk qualifies in my book as a writer."

If you are curious as to how books are written, this may be your best clue. Novelists don't simply sit down to write chapters only when the muses visit with inspiration. They've got notebooks full of scene ideas, rough dialogues, character lists, plot lists, and sentences that they wrote that seemed to have been said by someone a lot smarter than they are. The notebook may be the precursor to the published book. What is so valuable about this method is its flexibility. Actually, that's the value of each of these methods. You aren't locked in, you aren't married to it. You are trying things out, playing with your ideas and how to say them. This one, though, helps you over the weeks and months you will need to really get inside and underneath your ideas.

Reading (in Tandem with Freewriting or Brainstorming)

Yes, read on your subject, but don't stop with the Internet. Read books, magazines, journals; read the best thoughts on your subject. Get a sense of the field. And take accurate notes on what you read. Combine this with one or more of the other techniques above, especially freewriting. In fact, using freewriting, construct a dialogue between two of your authors or between two or three major points of view to get down on paper what is going on in your subject and what you know about it. Reading isn't just about getting information to regurgitate. It's about adding to your own voice some of the other voices on the subject.

By now, you might be getting the idea that there are different ways to kick-start your thinking, to, as it were, get your brain into the writing game. This is true. Here are some other suggestions that have worked in different ways for different people. Some are more visual than others—the first two probably help organize your thoughts.

Clustering

This is done by basically writing words in balloons around a paper. It is a return to elementary school in the highest sense, a special way of showing yourself, mainly, how your particular thinking on any topic is clustered into certain associations that may be different from other peoples' associations. To begin, write in the center of a blank page the word or words of a particular topic or subject you would like to explore further. Draw a small balloon around it. From there, what do you think of as you think about this topic? Draw a line in any direction, short or long, from the central balloon to the next word you think of. For example, the word "baseball" might lead to the words "steroid abuse." From here, you might think of Barry Bonds and Roger Clemens, so draw a line between "steroid abuse" and these two players' names. Further, you think of home run records and future inductions into the hall of fame; write these down and connect them to the appropriate names. You might think of the commissioner of baseball. Connect him to them. Next you think of Joe DiMaggio. Since he's not clearly connected to the current issue of steroid abuse, write his name closer to the original topic balloon, baseball, and draw a line between him and the main topic. On further thought, you may decide that the legendary Yankee whose record for consecutive games with a hit remains unchallenged and was accomplished without drugs (so far as we will ever know) makes for a good comparison to today's players, so you draw a second line between "Joe DiMaggio," "Barry Bonds," and "Roger Clements." As you can see just by this partial example, clustering can lead to the beginning of a focus. It can take a larger subject and show how thinking is clustered. It has helped certain authors to figure out the relationships between the chapters in books they were writing, and it has helped many writers to get a sense of their thinking about a difficult topic. The current cluster might be continued on a second page, with "steroid abuse" in the center of the page, and it might lead you to pick up on an actual focus or thesis, complete with topics you will develop further. Or it might not.

Outlining

This is one you've seen before. It may be considered the strapped-down cousin of clustering, but it is also much more famous, or infamous. For many high school graduates who don't go into writing or English, it sums up the entire subject. "I'm not good at English," I've heard them say, "because I'm not good at writing. I couldn't write an outline to save my life."

Outlining forces your hand about organization. It is as though your high school teacher had said, "I don't trust that you will be able to organize your thoughts, so here, do this first, and then write your paper." The problem with this approach, one your teacher should have known better than to insist on, is that, while it may get you thinking initially (that is good) about your topic, it may force you to order your thoughts before you know what they are. As a heuristic, outlining is great if it is only tentative and exploratory, if it includes several attempts and is not considered the final order. If it is final, as my high school teacher expected it to be, then it is nothing less than a straightjacket, designed to impede real thought and investigation, real writing that throws up new thoughts you hadn't been able to consider at the outlining stage, and research. It forces the linear game too early. Your readers like order, organization. But at this stage of the writing process, you aren't there yet. You aren't giving your reader anything yet. You are still playing. Like clustering, outlining does show an organizational pattern. But unlike clustering, it is linear, not spatial, not circling back to prior ideas for further development or consideration, for new suggestions of more interesting and insightful organizing principles.

The best use I've made of outlining is one I taught myself a decade after I'd finished high school English. Instead of outlining my paper before I wrote it (I'll admit I did a scratch outline—in my case, the scratch outline looks like a grocery list: see next section) I wrote a rough draft from start to finish. Then I read over what I'd written and, as I read, jotted an outline of the main chunks of thought that I'd done. I gave a word for each paragraph, and then I looked at this to see what my overarching thought was. On seeing the strange outline that emerged, I was able to see how I'd not developed certain ideas, over-reached on others, assumed certain ideas were true and provided no evidence, and went on tangents that finally were not connected to my thesis. The outline that emerged at this stage was useful in helping me to talk back to myself about my first draft and how I planned to really rewrite what I'd done. It showed me the areas that needed more construction. It showed me the way to develop my thoughts more. Outlining, in my own peculiar way of composing, is best used as a revision tool. To me, writing a formal, final outline before I write my paper is like asking me to write the table of contents to a book before I've started writing the book. That's fine, unless the table of contents is then immediately published and cannot be revised or strayed from. That was my high school teacher's view on it. The outline, set in stone, can't be altered or strayed from. This didn't work for me. At best, it told me to organize my thoughts. But at worst, it taught me that I had very few thoughts. It taught me to skip the invention stage altogether.

Scratch Outlining

These are my ticket into the writing process. Before I write, I'll either bring together freewrites I've done and think about them, or I'll jot down some order of appearance (sometimes I think of it like a performance, a variety show, rather than a paper, which seems so thin to me) on a piece of scratch paper, restaurant napkins or menus, scratchbooks given to me by realtors with their smiling faces on them, or lined notebook paper. This is my scratch outline. It is meant to get me thinking. I'll sometimes add to it, cross certain items out, and then add others. As I noted above, it may look no different from a grocery list, except that "Roger Clemens, Barry Bonds, hall of fame, caring for perceptions of twelve-year-old boys, we need a new commissioner" will not be found at the local grocer. The value of the scratch outline over the "formal" outline, as I've said, is that it gives a linear take, photograph on your thoughts, reminds you of where you are trying to go, and it is tentative and infinitely open to revision. It gives you the best of at least two worlds, the world of organization and the world of play. Both seem to be vital aids as we venture into the threatening chaos that is our own brains.

From the previous list, it might be useful to draw a few tentative generalizations. The best strategies you might use will be the ones that allow you to engage, at a maximum, your sense of play, of fooling around, and, at the same time, your sense of developing your ideas into something you can present to the adult marketplace of ideas. None of these ideas ever needs to be handed in, except as a record of where you've been, and only those that lead to ideas worth exploring more need to be used.

Some writers, especially those who find the process to be tedious, will decide that because nothing in these strategies is final or needs to be handed in, they won't try them out. This is deadly. There is a principle behind each one of these strategies, and if you don't do the strategies, you will miss the principle. You will not get better at your writing. Because you refused to allow yourself to be a kid and play a little, you won't make a very interesting adult. The stage of writing we call invention is a big, broad field that is not exhausted or fully defined by any one strategy, and there are a few other considerations to take up about them. But in each strategy we find the following principle: As I begin to write things down, I discover new things I want to say. Writing—freewriting, listing, brainstorming, outlining—has a generative quality. Writing leads to more writing, unless you've closed off what is appropriate to say. Unless you have a very restrictive teacher who expects only A, B, and C, writing before you write, playing, is going to lead to more writing and play. It will lead not only to D but also to L and that strange letter Q I've always wondered about. When this happens, what you do is talk to your teacher about L and Q. Are they appropriate? Or should they be left out? If they are appropriate, how can I tie them in? Dialoging with your instructors is always helpful to you as a writer.

To the above list, I'd add a few more below, because they take on a more obviously social tact and might be useful in showing you that you could take your ideas further.

Conversing

Yes, talk to others about ideas. Find out what they believe about your issue. You might find that you have only thought in clichés about your topic, that you haven't carried it beyond the most elementary stage of thinking. It could be that you've gone deeper than others, but hearing others talk about your idea could lead you to the common sense way people are engaging in the issue. This could give you an idea of how you want to write your introduction, starting with the common view, before you carry your reader further into the ideas you believe need to be considered. You may discover in conversing with friends that you actually disagree with them about certain things, and conversing with them about a topic for writing might help you to come up with a new argument to convince them that your view is worthy of consideration.

Dialoging/Arguing the Opposite of What You Believe

This is like the previous one, conversing, except that it is more formal and like a debate. It requires you to force yourself to take a position you may disagree with, think about how to defend it, and then make the best case you can for why it is right. The following three strategies are similar to this one, and you can do them alone or with your friends (or congenial adversaries).

Testing the Basis of Your Thinking

On a blank sheet of paper, write down what you believe about the topics you are thinking of writing about. Skip several lines to a half a page between each belief, conviction, or certainty you have written down. Then, below each, write in evidence for each. Include in that evidence everything that comes to mind. Then, look at your evidence. Do you need to read more to get more? Is your thinking not based firmly in evidence enough for others who don't share your convictions to accept it? For example, if you are taking a stand against euthanasia, are all of your arguments based on the Bible? If so, you may be very convincing when you argue with other members of your church. But in a university classroom, you will encounter others who don't read the Bible as an authoritative document. They will hear you as someone who is uninformed on the issue. What other reasons can you come up with?

As a second part of this strategy, write down any experiences you have had, positive or negative, with your topics. How might they color your thinking, and how might they be used as good examples to support your ideas?

Putting Your Ideas in an "Unnatural" Context

Again, the last two can be done in conversation with friends and teachers, with bosses and parents, with people on campus you've decided to talk to simply because they have very different experiences from you. These can be done socially.

Another aspect of this discussion of invention strategies is that it isn't the final word on the subject. Invention is a large subject. The philosopher Aristotle argued that invention made up the main topic of rhetoric. The first two-thirds of his book on the subject of rhetoric are concerned with invention. Style comes in with Book III, almost as an after-thought, something needed, but certainly not the main issue.

Chapter Summary

Though many assume that writing is something people are either gifted or not gifted at doing, learning to write well is still more than simply "having a knack" for it. It is, in fact, a subject that can be studied, and most people can learn to use writing to communicate. It may be that most people don't do the sorts of things that will help them to be successful with written communication. They assume that good, successful writers are, like Mozart, gifted people who never have to think about and invent their ideas before writing or write rough drafts that they then change in major ways. In contrast, this chapter makes the argument that many successful writers are like the composers Mozart or Beethoven. Some can write directly from the unconscious, while others, like Beethoven, must work hard, take notes, cross things out, and rewrite whole pieces before getting it right. Furthermore, it may be that when we are faced with new intellectual challenges, we may need more time to plan our ideas and rewrite them—it may be that we are more like Beethoven with these new challenges than Mozart, someone who has a whole vision of an idea and can simply write it down in one sitting. Given that this is the case, a list of strategies for getting started on developing ideas are given in this chapter.

Works Cited

Emig, Janet. *The Web of Meaning: Essays on Writing, Teaching, Learning, and Thinking*. Portsmouth: Heinemann, 1983.
Spender, Stephen. *The Making of a Poem*. New York: Norton, 1962.

Discussion Questions

1. Interview one of your teachers. What did you find out about your teachers and writing? List the assumptions you hold about writing that were confirmed by their answers. List the assumptions you hold that were challenged. Be prepared to discuss this as a class.
2. As a response to the ideas in this chapter, write a brief account of yourself as a writer, using the terms discussed here. Specify changes you'd like to address as you take this course.

Writing Assignment 1

on First Pretexts:
Writing Attitude Survey/Writing Prompt

Here is your first research into writing as a subject. To begin, journal or write reflectively on your answers to the following questions.

1. What are your first thoughts about the ideas in this chapter?

2. Is everyone a writer?

3. Can everyone learn to at least write well enough to communicate?

4. Where and when do good writers begin? The night before a paper is due? Do they plan what they have to say before they write?

5. Do "real writers," whoever they are, find writing to be easy?

6. Do good writers revise?

7. Does someone have the magic formula that whisks away every problem and makes writing as easy as eating a fast food hamburger?

8. What "strategies" do I use right now when I am given a writing assignment?

Consider your answers to these questions not as absolutes but as reflections of your current attitudes toward writing. Use your writing in response to these questions to reflect on the material presented in this chapter about writing process and invention.

Next, after you've gotten your ideas down, think about your previous writing classes. Think about an influential teacher you had. As I did at the beginning of this chapter, shape out a narrative of what you did in that class. Did you learn any of the ideas we've discussed in this chapter about writing? As you reflect on what you did in this writing class, think about what this chapter characterizes as the Mozartian/Beethovian distinction. In terms of your own experiences as a writer in the class you had with your influential teacher, has either or both of these categories ever been true of you? Did you ever find something simply pouring out of you? What was it? Did you ever find writing to be a real labor? What was the assignment, and what might you do to address this in the future?

Use your narrative of your classroom and the attitudes you unearthed in response to the questions above to compose a narrative for class, a writer's profile. End your essay with ways that you will want to change your writing. Think about new strategies raised in class or in this chapter that will allow you to practice writing by using invention.

Group Think

This activity has six parts.

Part 1

Do this alone. Make one list. Spend about five or ten minutes in class drawing up a possible list of topics you would like to develop more. After you've done this, draw up a second list of topics you would like to write about.

Part 2

After you've made the list in part 1, move to a group of four people. Go around the group and have each person read the first item on their list. If it is also on yours, put a single line at the end of it. For every time another group member reads it as being on his or her list, put another line by it. Do this, going around to each group member until everyone has read all of the items on his or her list.

Part 3

Note how often your ideas were also other people's ideas too. Compile a list of the topics everyone in your group came up with, noting where on the list they appeared. Were the first ideas you had also ideas that other people had? Did your blog list get more in depth? Or were your blog topics the same as everyone else's?

Part 4

Move to the whole class. Compare the list your group made for part 3 with the lists the other groups made.

Part 5

What do you learn about the first ideas you get? The later ideas that come to you, those in the second list? Does making a list of topics serve you well in thinking about things to write about? Why or why not?

Part 6

This was an experiment in invention. How well did it work? What else might you do?

feature 1.5   Writing Prompt Reflection

Having read this chapter, write a response to it. Do you agree that writing is a subject? What does this mean? Is writing a subject like history, with content to memorize? Or is writing something else, perhaps more like drawing or swimming? Explain and defend your commentary—write your own blog—giving examples and citing from Chapter 1.

Grammar Interlude 1: Nouns

Part of writing well for an audience includes using the grammar your audience knows. So, here is the first small component of that common grammar...

NOUNS

Why knowing about them matters to a writer . . . A style and grammar choice . . .

Most elementary school teachers stress adjectives and adverbs as important to descriptive writing. However, most college teachers stress that nouns are more important to a good style than adjectives or adverbs. Thingness and pictures in your writing come from concrete, well-chosen names of things in the world. Sacking them up with adjectives that come before them drains their strength.

Of course, you will say, you know what a noun is. It is the subject of the sentence. Okay. But nouns also appear in other ways in English sentences.

Please read through and do the following. Then comment on it by responding to the questions that follow.

Nouns Traditionally Defined

A noun names a person, place, thing, or idea. Nouns are typically understood as the subject of the sentence—whom or what the sentence concerns—who is acting or being . . .

Typical nouns include . . . apple, book, cow, CD, DVD, TV, pie, street, tree, Sarah, Luke (the last two are proper nouns, names of people or cities or schools that must be capitalized).

EX. 1. List five of your own nouns here. Mix in at least one proper noun:

1.
2.
3.
4.
5.

In a typical sentence, the subject will usually be a noun. BUT
What sometimes fools people is that nouns can appear in the later stages of a sentence as objects of action or as qualities complementing the subject.

For example, "**Luke** burned the **CD** at band **camp**." (In this sentence, "Luke," a proper noun, is the subject, the one who did the burning. But "CD" and "camp" are also nouns in this sentence. "CD" is a direct object—it is the object of Luke's action—burning—and "camp" is the name of the place or event where Luke did his burning. It is the object of a preposition, "at.") Don't be mistaken into assuming that a noun late in the sentence is the subject of the sentence. In English, the subject usually appears first, unless a modifying word, phrase, or dependent clause comes before it.

EX 2. Choose three passages from your reading. Underline all nouns. Circle all subjects of the sentences. (These passages should be handwritten by you and submitted to your teacher following this page.)

QUESTIONS FOR REFLECTION AND PRACTICE

What did you gain here?
Do these routines teach you anything of value for your own writing?
If so, what?
What will you do to connect with your future style and editing choices?

Chapter *Two*

Pretexts on Organization

Chapter Overview

Most people assume that good writing has a clear organization. But what is the best way to think about organization? Should there be pre-existing forms into which we simply force our ideas? Or should our ideas, our purpose, and audience determine organization for an essay? This chapter challenges some of the thinking surrounding the five paragraph-theme and suggests better ways to deepen thinking about organization. The most important point here is that organization is best thought of as tied to concerns with invention.

How I Spent My Between-Summer-Vacations

Some people confuse the organization of a piece of writing with what it is supposed to have as a purpose. In a piece of writing, the organization is the form or pattern around which ideas are organized. The purpose is the main role a particular essay, letter, or story is performing in the lives of the readers it is intended for.

For the following chapter, separating organization and function is meant to help readers understand each. Exploring options available to writers in beginnings, middles, and endings can lead to a discussion of why writers might choose the options they do. As with Chapter One, where the focus was placed on invention, this discussion in Chapter Two is one of strategies—or perhaps tools would be the better analogy. Following the horror novelist Stephen King, we are looking for tools for our writer's tool box.

feature 2.1   Writing Prompt 2

On the Five-Paragraph Theme—Five Uneven Paragraphs to Share with a Previous Teacher

College writing teachers sometimes refer to genres of writing that are "school based," meaning that the form is popular as a school exercise, but rarely or never seen elsewhere. The five-paragraph theme falls into this genre.

But if this is true of the five-paragraph theme and other assignments like it, some will ask, why is it taught so widely as a requirement? Who reads it? A key to answering the first question is found in the second. The main readers of the five-paragraph theme are the teachers who assign them. Because for a teacher who has between one and two hundred of them to read in a weekend, the five-paragraph theme is easy to grade. Why write it then? Because it makes teachers' jobs easy?

Those teachers who are most enthusiastic in teaching the five-paragraph theme argue that it does give students a structure to build their ideas on. It is a start.

The trouble with this argument, however, comes when we don't teach any other ideas about writing essays. It would be the same as if Beethoven had been taught the ABA song format but never had sonata or rondo form demonstrated to him. Sure, he was gifted, but even the gifted need to be given more than basic information. To draw on another academic field, learning only the five-paragraph theme would be tantamount to Einstein or Newton learning basic math—nothing beyond long division—and then being expected to become great scientists. In fact, as these comparisons show, when we teach writing this way, we seem to assume that if a person is gifted, then that person needs no formal instruction. If someone is gifted at writing, they don't need us teaching them. They already intuitively know how.

This means, of course, that only the gifted will get by, and only if they are very lucky, in today's writing courses.

Mozart and Beethoven on Form

The discussion in the last chapter about Mozart and Beethoven concerned just one musical form, the symphony. Yet both Mozart and Beethoven, like most composers—and writers—also understood how to write in other forms. In fact, every composer, like most every writer, studies more than a single form. Part of every composer's or writer's challenge has to do with deciding the form or shape that a new idea will take. For composers, that means determining whether or not an idea is best expressed in sonata form, rondo, canon form, or as a song, a march, or a prelude. Not every idea is equally suited to every form. This is not how we think about writing, however, especially in high school, where the five-paragraph theme remains one of the most popular forms of writing taught in high school English. Some high school teachers will even insist that the form appears in the "real world," though there is little evidence for this claim. In fact, though widely taught, the five-paragraph theme is required by few college teachers, except as an organizing principle in an essay exam, where the focus is on how well students can repeat information as proof that they know it. Typical of writing that is "school sponsored" or "school based," the practice is popular as a school exercise but rarely seen elsewhere. The comparison-contrast essay, the book report, the research paper, and the five-paragraph theme all fall into this genre.

For writers, the question of form will have to do with something called genre, or kind of writing, which has to do with purpose and audience. What is the writer's purpose? Is it to argue? Is it to entertain? Is it to inform? In the following chapters of this book, we will adopt a few genres to discuss in their most general terms of beginning, middle, and end: the personal narrative, the opinion essay, the explanation, argument, and researched argument.

Consider that not every writing task requires the same intellectual involvement and therefore the same process or approach. For simple or familiar tasks, we might produce the form readily, without much thought. For new tasks, for complex ones, we need more room for reflection. Not every writing task can be accomplished by plugging ideas into the same form. Most ideas cannot be reduced to five paragraphs.

Building on the Lessons of the Five Paragraph Theme

The five paragraph theme is defended for the way it is supposed to teach writers to structure their ideas. It provides a single template for beginning an essay, writing the body of it, and ending it. Advocates argue that this template can then be built on as writers continue to develop. What actually happens, however, is that the template is treated as an end to be achieved—on the SAT writing test—

and this end is used as evidence of writing proficiency. Considering that this is what most students actually experience, the final section of this chapter offers practical suggestions for developing new strategies after the five paragraph theme has been learned.

However, before reducing our consideration of writing practice to just that, several larger points should be considered. To begin, most people write for many different purposes. The five paragraph template serves one: It is written to explain information. Teachers who assign only this form may not believe that their students will only have the one purpose for their writing—explaining ideas that require only three points. But they are not preparing students for the various purposes for writing in the world, each one requiring a different form. Again, teaching only one form for the essay is similar to teaching a composer like Beethoven only to write simple songs. In fact, he learned and studied many different musical forms, and we also might be called on to provide explanations for different reasons. We might need to explain information. We might need to illustrate a concept, or we might need to clarify a procedure, and in writing in the real world, we might be called on to include all three of these explanations in a single essay. We might, for example, need to explain the relationship between concepts—through an examination of causes and effects, for example, or through comparisons.

feature 2.2   Statue of Mozart

feature 2.3   Bust of Beethoven

And certainly, other purposes than explaining information exist. Some writers and speakers write to inspire an audience. Others write to cast blame. Stories are written for both of these purposes and, as well, to entertain. Then there are the more common forms of persuasion. We argue and debate policies, decisions, ethics, and positions. And this list of purposes—to explain, to inspire, to argue, to entertain—could be added to and cannot be achieved by learning only the simplest way of explaining information. In fact there is growing evidence that if we are not taught these other forms, when we are assigned to write one of them, we will default to what we know—and the five paragraph theme is never inspiring or persuasive. We need other forms to help us become proficient as writers and to perform these other tasks.

The various aims for writing are often grouped into three broad purposes: expression, which sometimes is divided into personal and literary expression; exposition, or explaining information, which, as noted above, is quite complicated; and persuasion. Each has to do with audience. The next chapter on personal narrative provides an introduction to writing the personal narrative, one of the most popular forms of expression, which puts emphasis on the language, ethos, or the emotions of the writer. But most writing, to be read, is not just a matter of self-expression. Exposition requires a focus on information, and persuasion involves the values of readers.

Exposition as an Aim

The purposes listed above—expression, explanation, persuasion—would seem to represent airtight categories, but in reality, they overlap. If I am explaining a concept, I might use personal narrative somewhere—perhaps as the introduction—to engage, entertain, and even persuade my reader that the concept I will explain is important, has some hidden points they may not have thought about before, and is worth taking their time to understand. Conversely, I might need to provide a clear explanation of a concept as part of my attempt to persuade my reader to my position. Most writing will involve us in more than one aim, though there might be one dominant aim supported and helped by secondary aims for certain parts of an essay. Again, this is an area where the five paragraph theme falls short, since it assumes only one aim for writing. In contrast, writing for an audience will have complexity.

Exposition requires certain conditions—focus, organization, and awareness of different audiences. Make the explanation too basic and the audience will quickly disengage. Make it too complex, or omit important steps in a procedure or understanding, and they will be lost. Many math books seem written by math experts for other math wizards. So do computer instructions. One instruction manual for a computer I bought went to great lengths to define the mouse and explain its functions. But then it omitted the explanation of a complex series of steps in setting up the word-processing software. I had to call the company's help line. Clearly, the writers of this manual did not understand their audience. And being an expert does not necessarily make one the best explainer of a procedure.

Writers engage in explanations of concepts, methods, procedures, and processes, and the following patterns can often assist them with these tasks.

feature 2.4   Various Frames

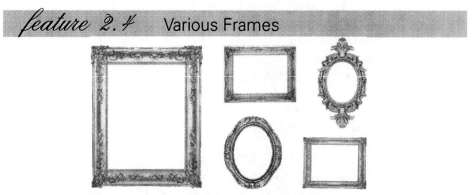

© 2009 by Nina Malyna. Used under license of Shutterstock, Inc.

Taking on Beethoven's Apprenticeship:
Various Patterns for Ideas

In addition to the five-paragraph theme, consider the following patterns by which writers are sometimes taught to develop expository writing. Obviously, the following list might be read as treating structure as the most important part of your writing process, and this isn't the case. It also places the focus on your practicing these forms, as though your whole point in writing is to learn the form, as though you will not ever write anything that doesn't require one of them, and this also simply isn't the case. You do not want to make structure more important than what you have to say. You want your structure to serve your aims for writing. The following is meant to offer alternatives, differing patterns and strategies for you to draw on so that when you encounter a writing prompt that challenges you, you can do more than default to your earlier training.

Please remember that these patterns are not meant to be treated as ends in themselves, as done with the five-paragraph theme. Rather, they are different options you have for both exploring a topic through invention, and for finally organizing an essay that has as its purpose conveying information to your readers.

Comparison/Contrast

This organizational pattern is somewhat reflective of how we think, especially when we are dealing with an unknown quantity. When the AIDS virus first began affecting populations in America in 1981, no one knew what this frightening new sickness was about. As information began to come out about it, sometimes it was expressed in comparisons. The AIDS virus was like other viruses in this way, but it was different in these other ways. By comparing a new, unknown quantity to what is already known, we increase our understanding. This is the strategy of poets when they write in metaphor or simile and compare an abstraction or an unknown quality to a well-known one. The comparisons can be enlightening.

Comparison/contrast is one scheme that allows you to compare two items, that is, to show how they are similar, and contrast them, that is, show how they are different. You can first compare them, showing their similarities, and then follow this with how they are different. Or, you can begin with their differences, and then show how similar they are. This depends on something that must inform every structure you choose, and that is your purpose for writing about something in the first place. If you keep hearing about how two political candidates are so different, but you see them as really being very much alike, you might begin an essay on them, if you want to get your point across, by showing that, yes, they are different, as everyone says. And then follow this with a contrast, such as, "However, more interesting than their differences are the simi-larities between these two candidates, especially in their stand on health care. Neither is proposing anything that different from the other. For example," and then list their similarities. Obviously, by beginning with their similarities, you are starting with where your reader is and showing them the common ground you share, even reminding them of this. That only serves to give the second part of your essay that much more impact. When you finish on how similar they really are, this is what you are leaving your reader with to think about.

There is one other variation on the comparison/contrast strategy, and it also should be considered in light of your reader's needs. Generally, writers can either write a block comparison or a point-by-point comparison. In a block com-parison, they first list all the points they wish to make about the first person, symphony, sports figure, or wing of a bird. After this, they present all of the same points about the other figure in the comparison. This, again, is called a block comparison. The first is usually given in a few paragraphs and developed. This is followed by a transition sentence, such as, "In contrast to the wing of the spar-row, the wing of the hummingbird has a muscular structure that allows for it's unusual flight patterns," or something along these lines.

The second pattern behind the comparison/contrast is a point-by-point comparison. This is typical of the plan outlined above where each paragraph covers certain points about each candidate, as in, "Our candidate clearly has had rich political experiences, both in Washington and as a state senator in New York, but the new candidate has been a senator also." Again, the pattern you choose should be determined by your reason for writing.

Cause/Effect—or Effect/Cause

This is used when the focus should be on causal reasoning. Often used in his-tory texts and in arguments on policy, the pattern allows the writer to outline for the reader how certain earlier events have led or will lead to certain causes. Refusing to study for an exam (event one), refusing to read the material to be tested on the exam (event two), and missing several classes where the most dif-ficult material was discussed (event three), are all causes, and you will argue that these causes will result in your friend failing the exam (the effect of these causes or events). From this, of course, you can then argue that this effect (fail-ing the exam) will become a cause (event) that leads to a new effect (having to go to summer school, or retake the course, or failure to graduate from college).

Some people, historians for example, might argue that some causes are more direct than others, that some causes have long-term and short-term effects. Many have argued, for example, that slavery was the main cause that led to the U.S. Civil War of 1860. Some have argued that the causes go further back, that, for example, the invention of the cotton gin made the growing of cotton more profitable, and with that, plantations increased their need for labor—of the most degrading and inhuman sort. Others, Abraham Lincoln, for example, seemed to suggest that literature was behind the war when he remarked, on meeting Harriet Beecher Stowe, the author of *Uncle Tom's Cabin,* "So you're the little lady who started the big war." The remark is, of course, sexist, but it also gives the author and a book a great deal of credit.

As practice and a form of exploration, consider doing the following: On a sheet of paper, map out a series of "If . . . then" equations or statements. On the left side of the paper, write down a list of causes; on the right side, list their effects.

1. What would be the effect on society if every taxpaying citizen were required to read at least five books a year? Conversely, what would be some of the effects if books suddenly were to be banned, or if they were to suddenly disappear and no longer exist.
2. What is the effect when the cause is fewer and fewer people turning out to vote in presidential elections?
3. Make a series of statements that begin with "What if . . ." Follow these with what you imagine their effects to be.

Listing

Not really a technical term, "listing" simply refers to having the writer follow an organization that is a list. Actually, this is the pattern that the five-paragraph theme appropriates in its design with "first, , , ," then, "second, . . ." and then "third, . . ." The trouble with its presence in the five-paragraph theme, of course, is that it becomes rigid (Only three reasons or issues? What about the others? I always wondered that—what about . . .) instead of something that helps you think about your reasoning about your subject and how you want to guide your reader. Typically, enumeration can begin with the least important or influential reasons or causes (yes, this one intersects with the last one) then build to the most important. Leaving your reader with the most compelling reasons for believing something is often a powerful way to organize your thoughts. Or, in contrast, you can begin with your most powerful, important reasons or causes, and then show how the others are not so important. Listing can be a the way to organize, depending on your purpose, though this is perhaps also a most basic way to organize your thoughts.

Process Narrative

This allows you to explain how a process works, either as a way of instruction—how do you use a new grammar-spell check in your computer?—or as a way of understanding how to fix something, as in how global warming really is occurring.

This pattern or structure can serve your purposes well. This might be similar to listing in that it is organized around steps that must be followed.

Narrative

This is the pattern of the story writer, novelist, nonfiction writer, or narrative poet, whose main focus is on telling a story in dramatic form. Usually, the narrative has a point to it, though the best writers in this form do not overstate the main point (some writers never actually state their main point). The narrative begins, as Aristotle wrote, *in media res,* that is, "in the middle," with an inciting incident (this captures the reader's interest). This is followed by rising action, a climax episode, and a (short) dénouement, or falling action. The narrative will often include dialogue between characters, description, setting, and character development, much of it achieved through dialogue. Some writers switch the parts of their narrative around, but the story can be used effectively to start an essay as well as be the entire focus of an essay.

Again, textbooks today often present these ideas as ways to structure whole essays, but they were originally devised to help with paragraph development. The danger for most writers comes when they mindlessly apply an organization without really reflecting very deeply on their subject. The purpose then becomes the pattern rather than the ideas you are communicating.

You can use these strategies either way. If you are making an argument, one of your points may come in paragraph five as a comparison between two political candidates you are arguing about. Or in paragraph three, you may want to explain the true causes of adult onset diabetes, though your larger concern is with a new kind of drug being offered by pharmaceutical corporations, whose main concern is always with making money. Does their concern help them to join you in your main concern, which is helping diabetics?

Practice

To practice some thinking about these patterns of organization, do the following. Get a sheet of paper out, write down the topic or thesis of something that concerns you. Then for each of the paragraph patterns above, jot down or write out ideas for each one. If you were to compare/contrast your ideas, what would you do? What ideas come to mind. Free write on this. When you are done, consider your idea in terms of cause/effect. After this, try enumeration, then process. Argue about it. Then tell a story.

Don't worry about form or polish here. The idea is to explore and expand on your ideas and to think about which form or forms might best serve your thinking and writing.

And Now, It's Your Turn to Be Beethoven . . .

If we are going to teach the five-paragraph theme as an introduction to structure, then we should also work in other structures, to build on what can be learned from the five -paragraph theme. And what do we learn from this form?

- First, it teaches that every essay or speech has a beginning, a middle, and an end. This is very clear.
- It is concise and simple.

But here's the flip side of bullet point 2, something else the five-paragraph theme teaches, and it's not a good lesson.

- It demands a narrow, simple format to this beginning, middle, and end. Though it is initially comforting to both teacher and student that not much thinking about form is required here beyond simply following the hard-and-fast rules, the form seems to require no discovery, no invention, just rote learning. Even the phrases that give the form its shape come ready-made for each paragraph.

I may have oversimplified things, but not by much. It is difficult to oversimplify a form that stresses structure over audience and over a writer's ideas. To become proficient writers, we also need to go beyond it. The following assignment builds on this prospect and offers a second way.

Writing the Five+-Paragraph Theme

Each of the requirements of the five-paragraph theme is absolute, though also arbitrary. Only five paragraphs? Only three middle paragraphs? What if your idea requires four paragraphs? Or what if your idea—like most ideas—requires not just "commentary," illustration, or evidence, but also modification, refutation, or some real extended development? And should you always begin with just one introductory paragraph? What about two? And what about that generic, "one size fits all" generalization at the start? Is that wise if you want to really capture your reader's interest? (Imagine, now we're talking about wisdom . . . What does that have to do with writing an essay?) Should you belabor for three or four sentences a boring "truth" or general blather about something your reader already knows?

For the following, as a test run into writing realms beyond the five-paragraph theme, your assignment is to write a five-paragraph theme. Or, you could skip this step, go back to Writing Prompt 2, and try to do the following steps by applying them to Writing Prompt 2. Or you could use the steps that follow and write your own personal essay.

Do this by plugging in a problem that you've been thinking about or one you've been discussing in class. Or write a parody of this form, and come up with an idea that will allow you to fully exploit it. Break your idea down into the format of this genre, and then when the ready-made phrases start to roll into your brain, write them down. For example,

In every life, they say, rain must fall. Sometimes that rain is hard and causes flooding, and other times that rain can be gentle and cleansing. But in every life, we must learn to take the harsh with the gentle and make the most of what life brings us. One way the rain falls has to do with how often people face strife at work. This strife can be harsh or gentle, but the main concern is with how the strife, or rain, is handled. In this essay, I will explain three ways of handling strife on the job, by exhibiting self-control, by not taking things personally, and by looking for positive solutions to negative problems.

This paragraph took me all of four minutes to write—more than one sentence per minute, and it pretty much serves the form, if nothing else. But in forming my introduction, I also have formed the rest of my essay, and this is potentially a positive value—unless I discover that my ideas are bigger than what I have initially mapped out here. But if I can keep my ideas fairly simple, I will have my pattern, and all of it is accomplished without any real thinking beyond what first comes to mind.

Although I may, as I continue to write or fill in the form, make new discoveries, the form itself will work to preclude this from happening, even not allow it. This is troubling, for often the very act of writing will show us deepening and revising our first conceptions. The act of writing might lead to a better formulation of our topic; it probably will show us that even though we are in the act of drafting our paper, we are actually still making discoveries about our topic. Nevertheless, the rule will be that anything that steps outside of the three points I've set up, even if they are important ideas, will have to be ignored. (Between you and me, I've often written these stray thoughts down and used them to rewrite a "better" five-paragraph theme later, if that is possible.)

Beethoven Writes Six Paragraphs . . .

After you've written your five-paragraph theme, your assignment is to read your work out loud to a group of your peers and your teacher. Once you've read it, get feedback. Is it "good" in fulfilling the assignment? What is good about it? What other ideas come to mind for you and your readers? Speculate with one another on other ideas that might help to deepen the essay and connect these to new ways to structure the old five-paragraph format, retaining perhaps only the beginning, middle, and end. Think about, in other words, ways to introduce new variations on this old format. Where might you play with the form and thereby make your writing more interesting? What aspects of the form can be changed?

The following I offer as a list that is not exhaustive. Please add more to it in your group. I offer it as a model of ways to build on what you've been taught.

1. Write a six-paragraph theme. Do this by either giving a two-paragraph introduction that begins with an anecdote about a specific person, place, or event, or by adding a paragraph to develop one of your three points—probably your most important point, which you will want emphasized—or by adding a fourth point that is needed. (If you or someone in your group asks, "Is this OK to do?" you really must do this assignment.)

2. Dispense with the concluding paragraph, trusting that the essay feels successfully concluded with the final point. Or drop the words "In conclusion" and the club or baseball bat restatement of thesis and main points and instead return to the anecdote or quote that you opened your essay with.

3. Consider that your three points are not all equally important and in need of seven sentences each, and instead write an argument about why one is the most important point to consider. Then think about a different order to your points. What should come first? Why?

4. Find an essay you really enjoyed reading and analyze its structure. What did the writer choose to do for an introduction? How was the middle organized? What did the writing conclude with? As a class, map out the various structures that you and your teacher discovered in these essays.

For each one of these suggestions you decide to work on, reflect on the following: How do the changes you made help your audience to be more captivated by your essay? How do the changes allow you as the writer to get closer to achieving your actual purposes for writing about your subject in the first place? In making the decisions you did, how much did your thinking about your writing change from how you thought about it as you wrote the five-paragraph theme? What was your focus for each of these? Compose your thoughts on these questions in a letter to your classmates and teacher. Be prepared to discuss them in class. Be prepared also to explain other ideas you have about improving on the five-paragraph theme, and to jot down the ideas you get from your colleagues in class.

Concerning Organization and Aims of Discourse: Chunks, Not Paragraphs

One other reason you were probably assigned the five-paragraph theme in high school will seem high-minded and even virtuous compared to the one about making grading easier, though it really only serves us as a beginning. I give this reason so late in this chapter because I am hoping that I have so discredited this form that I can now say something nice about it without appearing to support it.

The other reason your teacher taught the five-paragraph theme is that it was one way to give instruction in the paragraph itself, which in high school is generally considered the main unit of thought in writing. As most of us remember being told, a paragraph should consist of a single idea. This is a noble way to think, especially if it got us to try to develop our thoughts further than a simple slogan or generalization, or if it made us get specific and provide evidence. However, as a general rule, it simply isn't true. Paragraphs are probably best thought about not in terms of fixed rules, but of suggestions that are as open to revision and change as anything that is done in the real world for a real audience. The main proof for what I am arguing here will be found in those real world examples of writing in published books, magazines, journals, Web sites, and newspapers, where "real" paragraphs appear.

When you gather enough examples of these, either through coming together as a class or by looking at examples given by your teacher, consider that some paragraphs do not develop any ideas. The transition paragraph is the prime example of this. It exists only to guide your reader from point A in your essay to point B. It is about both point A and point B. Transition paragraphs also are not generally very long. In most cases, they don't usually deserve seven sentences of development.

Consider also that certain ideas need more than one paragraph for full development, that some ideas require four or five well-developed paragraphs. This happens. In fact, unlike the five-paragraph theme, all three kinds of para-graphs—the transition paragraph, the single-idea paragraph, and the five-idea paragraph all exist in the real world, where writers want to give their writing shape and power as they fully develop their thinking for their readers.

Consider also that different genres and audiences require different lengths of paragraphs. The rule for length in the newspaper paragraph stands at about one and a half sentences. The paragraph in academic writing among college researchers can often be anywhere from three quarters of a page to a page and a half long. This is because academics require extended evidence and discussion.

As we did with the five-paragraph theme, we might think about the paragraph as it was taught to us as a way to build on our understanding and deepen it. For-merly we were taught that the paragraph is a single unit of thought. Instead, we might think of several paragraphs as possibly coming together to form a single unit, which we might call a "chunk." These chunks represent stages of develop-ment in your essay, your thinking. A chunk might consist of a section of writing, over four paragraphs, in which you explain a new policy concerned with smoking in restaurants. Another chunk might consist of three paragraphs in which your introduction and thesis are developed. Another chunk might be two paragraphs where you give a response to an opposing argument. Think of your essay as consisting of stages of thought, or chunks of discourse. In fact, you might test this idea by outlining the different chunks in an essay your teacher has you look at.

Other Forms, Other Purposes, Other Genres

All too often with school-based writing, we are required to write in certain forms because they have been assigned by the teacher. Sometimes these forms are meant to teach us something about the kind of writing that is done in a given field. At other times, as with the five-paragraph theme, the reasoning is not so clear. Much college writing is assigned because it is assumed that as professionals we will need to write with these purposes in mind. Much writing has as its aim either exposition or persuasion. Exposition concerns the orderly and organized explanation of concepts, ideas, or bodies of knowledge—this amounts to an act of teaching in most cases. Exposition can also involve the detailing and analysis of experiences. In contrast, persuasion has as its aim not only giving information but also using information—as well as other appeals—to change people's minds and behaviors about issues where there may be more than one possible position.

Considering that both exposition and persuasion are widely required in college and will also be needed as skills for writing on the job, the following genres will be given consideration in the following pages: writing reports based on finding information, whether from surveys, interviews, or other ways of gathering data; writing arguments, whether short or longer and researched; writing analysis and evaluations, whether of popular culture (such as movies) or of programs of study or programs meant to help people; and writing personal accounts, such as profiles of influential people or of experiences that cast light on issues or topics of general interest.

These are some of the genres that will be explained and detailed in the following pages.

As always, we're assuming you've learned that to every work, there is a beginning, middle, and end.

feature 2.5   Writing Prompt Reflection

If you are still close enough to any of your high school teachers, show them Writing Prompt 2, the one that begins this chapter, and see what they have to say. Jot down their response and bring it to class. If nothing else, a writing class should encourage dialogue—even if it is after the fact.

Or, write your own blog for the Internet by responding to Writing Prompt 2 with the most important ideas in this chapter.

Grammar Interlude 2: Verbs

The second major part of speech—what helps, with the subject, to form the backbone, the action or statement of any sentence—is the verb. To put it in basic math terms:

SUBJECT (Noun) + VERB = CLAUSE

The Dark Knight + hid.

WHY VERBS MATTER . . .

With nouns, verbs are more important than adjectives and adverbs. They also make for pictures. Active verbs are powerful. With nouns, verbs form the backbone of a sentence.

There are three kinds of verbs to watch out for. Two are action verbs (transitive, intransitive), and one helps to express states of being.

Sleeps
Hits
Is

SLEEPS—Walter slept. "Slept" is the past tense of sleep. It is *intransitive*. That means that it needs no object to follow it to complete its action. You could say, "Walter slept on the cot," but "cot" is not needed. It's part of a prepositional phrase, but it isn't needed.

HITS—Walter hits. Wait, that doesn't work. Walter hits *what*? If you can ask "what," you have a transitive verb, a verb needing an object of its action.

***NOTE: -ing verbs become nouns**—swimming . . . running . . . reading— unless a linking verb appears first: "Sally was swimming" ("swimming" is a verb here), but "Swimming is hard" ("Swimming" is a noun here).

EX. 1. Go BACK TO EX. 1 in chapter 1. List five verbs to go with the nouns in that exercise.

EX. 2. In three passages from your own writing, select all verbs. (These passages should be handwritten by you and submitted to your instructor along with this page.)

QUESTIONS FOR REFLECTION AND PRACTICE

What knowledge did you gain here?
Do these routines teach you anything of value for your own writing?
If so, what?
What will you do to connect with your future style and editing choices?

Chapter *Three*

Writing from Personal Experience

Chapter Overview

Chapter 3 presents arguments about the relevance of personal writing to writing development. A discussion of various perspectives is followed by a thinking about how different forms of personal writing can be done. Two forms are explained, the personal narrative and the character profile. Explanations for approaching both assignments successfully are given.

Inquiry and Storytelling

Considering the issues raised about personal writing, the questions inevitably arise: What purposes, what aims, do stories serve? Do they belong in a writing class?

For most people, stories are entertaining. Some will not care to read the latest research on an important issue, but they will listen to stories about it. Everyone tells or listens for stories, but they do it for more than entertainment. Spinning tales makes us human, diverts us at the same time that it captures some sense of what it means to be human. Even scientists, when making their case for the triumph of rationality over superstition and the scientific method over religious devotion, tell stories. After all, the many retellings of Galileo's conflict with the church, though told by scientists, are still examples of storytelling, and meant to assert one set of values over another. Like these scientists, we tell stories to make points, to account for changes in our culture, and to help persuade others.

Religious speakers often use the broader appeal of the story "illustration" over theological analysis, perhaps for some of the same reasons scientists give accounts of Galileo. Narratives give meaning to what might otherwise be sepa-

feature 3.1   Writing Prompt 3

What's Wrong and Right with Personal Writing

Debate has centered recently on whether personal writing should be done in a writing course. Some teachers think that writing personal essays and narratives about issues students care about helps them to find their voice, which many teachers and students associate with identity. And, of course, some students enjoy writing about issues they care about or have strong feelings about, and they identify this with personal writing. On the other hand, some find personal writing to be self-indulgent, and they would rather have students think about who their audience is and issues that concern a larger context than just the self. At the farthest extreme of this view are those who would prefer simple reports drawn from research, with no mention of the writer or the writer's position evident anywhere in the paper. Some writers would prefer to do this. "Give me a subject," they say, "and I'll look up information on that and give it to you."

The forms personal writing can take vary from letter writing, keeping a journal, and narrative writing, to writing character accounts of people we admire. Some of these forms may not seem worthwhile in that the writer can start with personal, even selfish concerns. Indeed, to be successful eventually, he or she will sooner or later need to consider her audience. This means rereading over the ideas to make sure they are well developed and clear. It means checking the message for grammar error, unclear diction, or sentence patterns that are unwieldy. Certainly this is true of the letter, or even an e-mail—if you are sending an e-mail to your supervisor or a professor. It could also apply to a story or a character profile. In the final analysis, the writer of these forms must consider how to convey her ideas in such a way that an audience will respond to them. When doing this regarding subjects that are personal, students can often write with authority and purpose, owning the act of writing. This ownership, given some help, can sometimes—though not always—carry over into research writing and argumentation. Certainly, if framed the right way, a personal writing assignment can lead a writer into the beginnings of doing research. Grieving for a lost parent, spouse, or sibling can lead to research into grief and loss. Suffering from a sports injury can lead to research on health and medical issues.

If we think about personal writing in terms of inquiry, in terms of asking questions and wanting to make connections, these are the same terms by which we approach these other, seemingly less personal forms of writing.

rate, innert facts. Stories are also told at other kinds of public speaking venues—for example, when a university president delivers a message, a speaker addresses graduates at a graduation, or a politician addresses supporters. The quiet moments in a crowd come when everyone is listening to a story. The story is usually short, sometimes nothing more than an anecdote. But it has characters. It has plot and setting. It adds up to a significant point or illustration quickly, sometimes with brevity.

It is even the case that stories help us understand how the world works. Consider that many legal thrillers are read to find out what happens next in the plot, but also because the readers are interested in learning more about how the legal system works.

Considering the venues where stories are told might better help us determine why we tell them. Critics note that the market for literary short fiction is not strong; many journals that once published short stories have folded, and many magazines that once had a mainstay publishing short stories every week no longer do so. Furthermore, most published novels do not sell out of the first edition and are not read. For every best-selling novel, there are hundreds of unknown books that will go out of print. And yet the markets for popular, genre fiction—especially murder mystery, legal fiction, and romance—remain bulwarks of publishing. Consider that the biggest market for stories, however cheap or gaudy, is television. This bastion of advertising and reaffirming conventional ideas—from its countless repeated advertisements to its longest running soap operas—is built on story arch.

It is clear that narrative is alive. Whether it comes as an advertisement for a hamburger, or as a novel, a prose poem, a memoir, or a case study, the story is still around. It seems to adapt to every possible aim—from the most trite to the most lucrative. But it continues to be synonymous with being human. One of the ways that we try to make sense out of our lives is through telling and hearing stories. We tell them to connect with other humans. We use them to illustrate important points, even make them memorable. We tell stories to entertain. And through them, we can also convey information.

Beginning with the Personal

Writing that comes from experience as its beginning, as Michael Carter has noted, is writing that "heightens our awareness of experience" (21). As we begin to write about what has happened, we come to increased awareness of what we have gone through. This suggests the possibility that writers of personal experience are not merely being self-indulgent but possibly also engaging in reflection, in becoming more conscious of what they have experienced. Indeed, the best writing from personal experience will consist of two basic elements—a re-creation of the experience itself, and some aspect of reflection or analysis arising from the re-creation of the experience.

There is also a contradiction here that seems to run through the best writing from personal experience, especially creative nonfiction essays and fiction: The best personal writing moves the writer beyond the personal, makes her or him aware of communal connections. Also, in the best, most honest cases, the writer does not begin with a moral or a point to be made. He or she might do this to begin with, before revisions. But the best work results from those who allow their writing to speak back to them, to change their perspective, to allow the unfolding material to suggest its own center, its own better and more interesting point.

There is also the literary aspect of telling stories, which throws light on the language being used, or leads to an increasing awareness of beauty. By putting a focus on certain themes, the writer of experiences is open to those times when an account, for example, of getting a wallet stolen, can lead to reflection on identity or feelings of security. It's not that they are trying to make larger points about life. It's that the themes suggest themselves, are there in the material to begin with. But again, the writer's focus is still on getting ideas across through the use of words, on trying to communicate in language.

Some writers have also noticed that their experiences can change depending their personal commitments. Many creative nonfiction writers have powerful political commitments that come out in their stories, which also convey to us the importance of justice. The commitments for the writer are always changing and deepening, especially as writing leads to further reflection. At the same time that the actual details of what happened are finally revised into a careful selection and given a shape and design that is meaningful, the writer reaches a point of reflection and analysis that yields meaning. There is not only the conveying of the experience; there is, perhaps more importantly, the reflection on what the experience means. This second part, the reflection, is not the same thing as a moral to the story. It is not, as in the animal fable, a platitude or cliché that can be extracted from it. And it won't necessarily appear at the end, after the experience. It may, finally, get reflected in the word choice, in the ordering of the details as the writer attempts to capture what it means to be alive and human. This reflects a sense of community, an involvement that the writer of experiences finally understands. In this, the writer of personal experience does not descend deeper into the self and farther away from society; instead, she brings something rich and telling back to the conversation.

The following two assignments involve writing about experiences. The first, the narrative essay, is harder than it first appears. The second, the profile, also has its difficulties. Both might constitute the beginnings of research.

Writing the Personal Narrative

Writers of personal experience may seem not to need credentials to write what they know. This may be one reason why this kind of writing is popular. However, a pattern can be detected in writing about experience. Three different types of writer, to begin with, are pretty typical. The first is the reporter of personal experience. This person is actually a storyteller. His or her writing will be dramatized and presented in all of its detail, with good timing and narrative pace. The second type is the polemicist, the writer of essays who has a point or an ax to grind. This writer may begin with an experience, but it comes to represent something bigger and broader and leads to a larger, usually argumentative point. The third type likes to write about him- or herself for personal, therapeutic reasons. The ideas this individual works from are often deeply personal and elusive, but also ultimately fragmented and enigmatic, material with potential but not yet meant for a reader.

In all three cases, it has been my experience to hear people say that though they don't like to write, they do like to write personal narratives. They like to write journal entries. The need here to be reflective, to jot down something of what has happened, is strong enough to motivate them to certain forms of writing. Perhaps least compelling, however, is the writer who views writing as a form of therapy. This is all fine as far as it goes, certainly, but this is also not the kind of writing that will be meaningfully shared with anyone other than a therapist. Something else—some emotion, a feeling of well-being, an understanding of the self—is more important to these writers than connecting with readers. The best writing from personal experience, in contrast to this, can begin when this real desire to get to the core of an experience intersects with a similar desire to communicate that core to others in ways that are not clichéd or motivated for personal, mental health concerns. This can happen to the writer of therapy when she or he ceases to think in psychological terms and begins to think in literary terms of themes and motifs. Then, the deeply personal can be the stuff of fiction, poetry, and creative nonfiction. And this move, from our private reflections, to having something to say to others, is not exhibitionist or self-involved. The more we try to make our ideas clear to others, the more we understand what they need to hear.

Beginning in the Middle?

There are a number of ways to begin writing about our experiences. The material we draw from ourselves can be mundane, trivial, disturbed, or full of excitement, but it is what we then do with it in the craft of storytelling that will determine its final interest for us and for others. In reflecting on whatever images or experiences are in our thoughts as we begin to generate ideas and work at our invention, in a free write or a journal entry, we might write these down as clearly as possible, exploring what they might mean. But it is quite important not to make snap judgments, to decide that nothing we've experienced is good enough. It is important that we get everything we possibly can out on the table for our reflection. Keep in mind that it is not just the story itself we are telling but also the slant we plan to tell it in. That slant can be one we take to the writing of it, or it can be something that emerges as we listen to the details of our story.

This point is important. Though we are writing about our own experiences, we should keep our eyes open for the patterns that emerge from the details and the larger implications in them. What do they imply for giving our experiences a larger context, however mundane the details might be?

Another approach that might be taken to personal experience might be to write about an experience you've wanted to get down, for whatever reason. To do this, pay attention to what the experience wants to tell you. You might begin with an experience that captures the first time you noticed that you were different from others in some important way. Don't focus only on how that made you feel, but also on how it made your friends react. Imagine discovering that you liked classical music or musicals instead of hip-hop. What would that do to your relationships? Concerning the handling of this theme, read Lisa Louie's essay, which appears at the end of this chapter. Notice how she portrays two very different motivations she experienced in middle school—popularity and being a band geek—and how these eventually were brought into conflict when she was asked to play her saxophone for an assembly.

There are a number of firsts that can be explored for material. Think about your first job. How did it challenge you or your beliefs? How did it make you different? What were things like for you before you started working? What were your attitudes toward work? How did they change afterwards? Did anything happen on the job that made you think about and reflect critically on American values? Or reaffirm them?

Obviously, the first issue here will be to get down in as much detail as possible what happened. Your reader will be interested in finding out what happened. They will want to live through your experience, so you will want to shape your narrative in such a way that it begins with an inciting incident and then rises in tension through conflict before it is finally resolved. You will want to capture conversations as well as the way people looked and talked. You will want to give your reader a sense of place, or setting, though in a meaningful way that is revealed in the course of the action, and not given statically. Our method of storytelling has changed since the nineteenth century, when Henry James could spend an entire opening chapter simply describing the furniture in a room before any characters appeared in it. Today, you will need to begin with the characters themselves.

Scene and Summary: Focusing on a Narrative

The narrative writer has several tools to use. Scene and summary can be seen as the way to building a compelling and focused story. Thoughtful reflection can deepen it.

The scene is the place where the action happens. In writing scenes, the focus in placed on those moments in the story when something happened, when two or three characters talked to each other and tried to influence each other. Scenes are typically shaped by dialogue. Every story has these, and they are the place where the story is given its focus. Many narratives will start with a scene of action, with the opening moment when the writer learned something was wrong with his friend. It then recounts how he reacted and what he did.

The scene is what makes the story worth reading.

In contrast, the summary can cover days, weeks, even years that pass before the next important event in the story takes place. The summary can serve as a kind of transition to stitch events together and can consist of a mere phrase, as in "The next day..." or "Two days later..." or even "Over the next five years..." These convey the passing time that doesn't matter to the story, and they help the writer get back to the real focus of the actions that matter to the story.

As an example of a skilled use of scene and story, consider a short personal essay by David Sedaris called "Let it Snow." This essay of about five pages recounts how Sedaris and his sisters were kicked out of his mother's house during a long series of snow days. The first part of the story goes between scenes in which the children try to get their mother's attention in order to get back inside and summary of the hours that pass between those attempts. The scenes have dialogues in which the characters interact, insult their mother, and make plans. The summary is simply this: "My sisters and I went down the hill and sledded with other children from the neighborhood. A few hours later we returned home, surprised to find that the door was still locked." The summary is found in the one line, "A few hours later we returned home..." It covers several hours, but it allows Sedaris to focus on the main story without giving tangents about children on sleds and toboggans. Moving between scene and summary, the story builds to a moment when their mother comes out to take them back home.

Lisa Louie's essay, reprinted at the end of this chapter, begins with a short, momentous scene in which she shows herself taking apart her saxophone at the end of band class, and doing so slowly to avoid being seen in the halls outside by her more popular friends. This scene is followed by some reflection on popularity in middle school, and then, in the seventh paragraph, a summary: "By eighth grade, I had grown comfortable around these girls who laughed like hyenas and rotated through boyfriends with each other, sharing them like bags of popcorn." And then, she begins a scene: "Once, during lunch, when we were all huddled in the bathroom..." The scene that follows is a short dialogue that captures her friends in their most characteristic moments:

"'Did you know that there is a right and a wrong way to wear a belt?' I asked...

They were interested. 'What do you mean?' one of the girls asked...

'Oh, I was just noticing that you have to go through the left belt loop first or else the design is upside down.'

They all considered this for a moment and then simultaneously checked their own belt to make sure it was put on the proper way. In that moment as I watched them, I felt like the greatest authority on fashion. I had taught them something, and without question they had followed."

This short scene reveals character, it shows why the narrator valued these friends, and it deepens the conflict she feels between winning their approval and also wanting to explore music more deeply, an interest they would clearly not share.

In these examples, Sedaris and Louie move between scene, summary, and reflection to build a central focus and conflict.

Narrative and Reflection

Reflection or analysis on the theme, that other aspect of your story, will be harder to convey, but as you get down what happened and think about why it matters that you tell it in the way that you do, you might start to reflect on what it means. The best experiences to write about are those that reveal some inconsistency in the way we think about certain issues—for example, how we are told to value ourselves over others, or how we are told to honor our parents, or how we are driven to find the acceptance of others. In these stories, we don't tell our readers that the story we are writing is about a certain inconsistency. We show the inconsistency itself. We show ourselves in tension. Each of us will experience these tensions differently, whether it's the tension between being loyal to our friends and gaining something for ourselves, or the tension between doing what is right and doing something that makes us popular. The best nonfiction narratives are those that capture these tensions at a deep level that suggests where we are at culturally in the present moment. The fact, for example, that you might tell about doing things to be popular could be because you want to reflect ironically on how this is no longer a big deal—in fact, who wouldn't want to fit in? Your final tone in your piece, your final meaning, may have to do with some other position than a traditionally moral one. As one example, George Orwell's essay "On Shooting the Elephant," dramatizes the way the pressure he felt in his surroundings led to his shooting an elephant to gain approval. The action itself rises to the level of being a critique of Western colonial imperialism, though Orwell never comes out and says this directly.

This is writing that is not arrived at the first time. The attempt at authenticity is really many attempts, revisions.

It should be acknowledged that the narrative essay is sometimes read by our colleagues in other departments—in the sciences, in sociology, in philosophy and theology—as soft, even self-indulgent writing. Developing your skills as a narrative writer will not help you in other classes. You probably won't be asked to write narratives again, unless you take creative writing. But this does not mean it is not important. Obviously, narrative still has its place in our culture, and there are important things to be learned from writing stories. Pay attention to how language emerges as you write, and pay attention to the way that writing a narrative almost forces you to be a more careful observer than you would otherwise be. Pay attention to how your awareness of your experiences changes as you write about them. Writing incites reflection.

For Starters

A photographer notes that when he first became interested in photography, he took a class in it in college. The instructor opened the class with the following advice: "Now that you have your cameras," he said, "go ahead. Go out and get all of those sunset-at-the-beach pictures out of your system. Take all the cute puppy and cute baby shots you think you need to. And when you're done with all of those, come back, and we'll start talking about seeing as a photographer. The history of photography is bigger than the greeting card store on the corner. Some photographers have shown us the Grand Canyon, of course, and others have used their pictures to instigate social and industrial labor reforms. When you've done one too many of your sunsets, when the forth or fifth starts to feel old, come back and we'll start talking about where your real pictures are going to be found."

This photography teacher was used to new students all seeing the same things and taking the same pictures. We call these clichés. There is probably some deep reason cliché happens. It probably emerges from the same community well as most commonplaces do. But as this teacher was saying, for any who would listen, the difference between the casual tourist with a camera and the real photographer comes down to this: The tourist gets her camera out only on a trip and sees what has already been shown to her; the photographer sees what is there, which is always something more than what has been shown to us, something peculiar. One follows others' visions, and the other has started to learn to see.

The same is true of the narrative writer. We might begin by getting all of your car accident stories, or your "first kiss" or "first crush on a boy" love stories out of your system. Write them all out, and then come, sit down again, and we'll get started on the stories that really matter to us. Clichés abound in too much writing today—especially on television and in movies. One way to get away from them is to read more and watch TV less.

Among the clichés we might first choose are the stories concerning a major event. The trouble is that a major life event does not always equal a good story. A major event, for example, might be high school graduation, a car accident, or the first time we had an emotional experience in a relationship. The trouble with these is that writing about them shrinks them somehow. What is there to say about our graduation beyond waiting in line, hearing our name read, and getting pictures taken with friends? Where is the story in this? And while we may think that a car accident we were in will be a good topic, it often doesn't take us far. After the narration of the wreck, the point of these stories seems to get lost on the writer—unless they begin to reflect on what the automobile has done to change how we think about our lives and how a car wreck epitomizes the hurried way we live and die. But even this seems a bit clichéd now. Perhaps it's best to keep the graduation, car chase/wreck, and the first kiss stories for the movies.

Similarly, a death in the family might seem important, but often these are written as tributes to the deceased, and too often they are sentimentalized. The real point isn't there beyond the therapeutic good it does the writer. Or the story might be of some value to the writer's family. But it won't really get at the heart of why someone's death was worth writing about.

Each of these "big" experiences, of course, might make a worthwhile narrative, but they will also be tricky to write about. Ask yourself why you are writing it. If you are doing it for a reason that finally does not lead you to consider the reader, you probably are not ready to write about it. The key is to get at the stories that we really must tell, even the ones that might seem unpromising at first, that don't concern a big event, even stories that do not put us in our best light. These might be stories about when we didn't feel so well, weren't in our top form, or didn't look better than others—stories about the sage or commonplace advice that did not lead to success. Write about these. Then think about what there is to learn from them.

feature 3.2

© fantasista, 2009. Used under license from Shutterstock, Inc.

Observation: One Important Skill Gained from Personal Reflection

One aspect of ourselves that is sharpened in narrative writing concerns observation. Every writer, regardless of whether she is a sports writer, a novelist, a business writer, or a poet, develops and fine-tunes the art of observation. She majors in all that this entails. The writer pays attention to the world around her or him, noticing details that others will overlook as unimportant. And she will refuse to draw quick conclusions, often curious to know more about causes and effects. A part of the writer's powers of observation involve noticing how she reacts to the details she sees: She questions what in her observations will lead her to draw the conclusions she does. Are those conclusions the logical ones to draw? The writer, then, is a keen observer of both herself and others, a listener before she is a talker.

Along with being a careful observer, every writer reflects on the conclusions she draws from observations. She becomes thoughtful about how her observations and conclusions reflect a personal perspective of values. We become aware of how we are taking in the world around us. We think about the things we notice, and we think about what we conclude from what we notice. The rest of the time, when we are not focused on our own observations, these details and conclusions will be invisible to us, and we won't be aware of our own thinking—our own prejudices and preferences. But as we focus on this, we become more conscious of them.

Both of these ideas concerning observation and reflection involve, at an immediate level, our thinking process and our cultural outlook, both of which remain invisible to us, unless we are confronted with them. They involve our ideology and that of others. Very few of us will stop to listen to how we are taking in a scene in front of us. As we are involved as an observer, we may be quick to draw conclusions. Those conclusions are what we are interested in, as they have to do with our personal values and our community ones as well.

For purposes of discussion, I would like to simplify the structure of how we observe into two parts. Consider that in every observation there are first the details that are noticed, and then there is the conclusion that we draw from them. Both parts, both what is noticed and the conclusion, will be determined by our particular individuality, or framework. What determines our framework will usually be our past experiences, but also our communities, our gender, race, and religious values. We rarely step outside of our own expectations to be careful observers. It is important to try to notice what is really going on, to really make the first part of the structure better, and not just fall into what fits with our predetermined expectations.

Starters: Dealing with Crowds, People, Ourselves as Observers

A coffee shop, diner, or your local college student center and eatery all represent full semiotic streams teaming with signs and details rich in suggestion. Even so, we begin to edit and become selective in our observations the moment we enter them. Yet even the local college eatery, patronized mostly by members of your school—faculty, students, and staff—is more diverse that you might think. As one practice, plan to go there, or to a local café, get a table, and to do two things.

- First, write down everything that *you* notice, everything that seems to matter to you. Draw as many conclusions about these details as seem warranted.
- Second, eavesdrop on a conversation. Note first your observations, your first reactions to the people around you. Jot down your first impressions (probably rich with your ideology). In doing this, be sure to include not just your conclusion or your assessment of them, but also the details that lead you to your conclusion. For example, "Middle-aged man in sweat suit could be a

feature 3.3   Man and Woman Eyeing Each Other

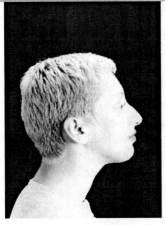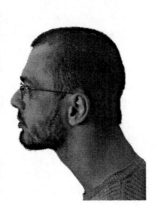

© Dimitri, 2009. Used under license from Shutterstock, Inc.

professor working out on his office hour." Include the appearance (middle aged and wearing a sweat suit) and your assessment (professor working out after class). Then get down as much as you can of a conversation taking place near you. How do people say things? What do they say? What do you learn about them that confirms your observations? What is new?

Writing the Essay

To this point, this chapter has been concerned with writing from experience by casting it as narrative. This is the attempt to re-create experiences for a reader, though this attempt also has the quality of bringing us to reflect on our experiences through the words we choose. There is value in both of these things. Another form of writing also drawn from personal concerns is the thematic essay, which may include narrative accounts or personal experiences, but the main structural and organizing feature of it is not one single narrative. Instead, the personal essay can focus around a theme or an image that the writer develops through a series of events and reflections, or even a combination of reported events and reading done on the subject. Especially if the writer has been influenced by another writer on a given subject, bringing in what this other writer has to say can deepen our reflection. In fact, it could be that the narrative essay you wrote for the first part of this chapter on personal experience constitutes just one stage, one section, in a longer, more thematic account, one that allows you to focus on your theme more completely.

Writing the personal essay is rewarding for connection it can bring between ourselves, our thinking, and others. The first benefit, of course, is the clarity it can bring to our own thinking as we seek to develop it more, to try to see connections between things we've experienced, the reading we've done, and the images that matter when we think about an issue. Perhaps a primary, short, powerful example of this kind of writing would be Annie Dillard's "Living Like Weasels," one in which her brief account of encountering a weasel on the edge of her suburb is followed by a meditation on the animal, including an account she gets from her reading, of a weasel attaching itself to a bird of prey that has caught it. Again, what she has experienced has led to connections that deepen her account and allow her to develop her real theme, which is this: What the weasel can teach us about living intensely in the moment.

Perhaps you may be left cold by Dillard's rhapsodic account, especially if glimpses of the natural world do not excite you as they do her. Perhaps a better start for you might come with reflecting on your relationships and experiences as a student. Perhaps a better starting point comes when you reflect on technology, starting with your use of it. None of this matters. What matters is that you start with a point that is common to others, one that you explain in some detail, bringing your readers to a place where they can see your point of view on it.

Begin as we do in the first part of this chapter. Think about an experience you've had, and write it down. After that, reflect and free write on what this experience means to you. As you reflect, consider the larger issues in a nonclichéd way, and consider how the theme you are discovering can be developed more.

The Thesis Statement in Personal Narrative

It is, of course, true that a personal narrative, or the more personal essay just described, will probably not contain an actual thesis statement in the text, certainly not like one found in an argument. Yet a personal essay always has a focus whether stated directly or not. Most often, the main point is implied by the action of the story and the theme. One good way to think about your main point and also about revising your personal narrative is to think about the themes that come up in your story. For example, is your story about father-son relationships? What does it seem to be suggesting about them? This leads you to understanding the main point of your personal essay. It does not mean that you should then, in a later draft, place a thematic statement in the essay. But it does help you understand your real purpose for writing, and in successive drafts, you should try to bring out more details that support and deepen your main theme, or as is the case in many narratives, themes.

Profiles

Profiles represent one form of writing that seems concerned with values and personal experiences. To do research for them, the writer must either conduct interviews with the subject or read biographies. Written for a variety of purposes and audiences, the character profile is perhaps frequently enough written for inspiration. John F. Kennedy's *Profiles in Courage* is one example of this, though there are many more. Obviously, limitations for the writer in terms of space and time mean that the writer of a profile must focus. It is not possible to say everything there is to know about a subject. Perhaps the writer will focus on her subject's career moves. Or she will focus on her subject's beliefs and how they have been shaped by one or two key events in her life story. Some profiles are actually used in psychological research, where patterns are predicted and found in common with other profiles.

What can we learn about writing from composing lives of other people? The profile, as outlined here, calls on you to do two things: First, you must conduct a successful interview to gain your information; second, you must compose your findings into a focused article of interest to readers for some reason. For one kind of profile, the focus can be to learn something about the values of a person who does not belong to your immediate community. This person's values are actually quite different from your own, and your work involves your listening to their story and suspending judgment, and instead, asking further questions for clarification. Your concern here is with making this person of interest and clear to an audience of your peers.

As with narrative, the features of a profile will first focus on developing the subject of the profile in as much detail. This concerns aspects of character. As with a good narrative, character is revealed to us as we observe carefully, paying attention to the way that people talk, the recurring patterns of words they use, the subjects that they often return to. (Note: If you want to get your subject really talking, show them you are interested in what interests them. Don't try to "find common ground." This is their film.) Character is also revealed by the things other people say about them. You might be able to find this out from your subject, though you also might bring others into your profile.

Character is revealed by action, as Aristotle asserted. But we can also learn about people by hearing their background. Some questions can concern where someone was born, where they grew up and went to school or church, what their parents did, what their family was like, what they thought about dating. As a person's background emerges, the story or the focus will also emerge, giving the writer a clear sense of what to focus on. The better questions are those that get a subject talking, perhaps open-ended questions. Obviously, since most people are not always direct or computational in their response to every question, the

feature 3.4   Sundown Cowboy

© Robin Holden, Jr., 2009. Used under license from Shutterstock, Inc.

writer of a profile should stay open to hearing answers to certain questions that come from thinking about other questions. The following is a breakdown on different areas of a person's life that you might use to devise questions:

Life Story—history, background—birth, family background, siblings, parents, grandparents, ethnicity, religion, stories about growing up that are revealing
Professional Life—education, career—where education, interests that led to work, stories
Beliefs and Values—issues that come up for them—what they most value, what they believe about life, what they believe about people?
Pet Peeves—things that are upsetting—what gets them angry, what gets them talking, what they see as wrong and right

In addition to these, the profile writer must answer this question: Why should we care about the person being profiled? It is the writer's job to give the reader good reasons to care. Obviously, direct questions like "What do you most value?" may not lead a subject to talk about what they most value. But it is vital to be on the lookout for recurring interests or people or things that come up in an interview. In your profile, you will want to capture the subject's voice in addition to your own. You will want to capture a focused picture of them in their most typical surroundings doing things that are most typical of them. For example, if you are interviewing a firefighter, you will want to capture them on the job at the station, lifting weights or playing cards or sleeping. If they are an office manager, you will want to capture them at the office, in their element, giving the most telling details about their office—pictures of family, friends, associates, awards, posters, artwork, objects that reveal something about them and lead to a story, to a discussion of values. Try to capture what they disagree with.

In contrast to their work environment, what about home? How is home different from work for them? What is their family life like, and are they satisfied with work, with family? Why, and why not? What more do they want? What did they start out wanting, and how did that change?

Yet another question might concern their contradictions. To be human is to be inconsistent, and everyone can be found to state a certain set of beliefs—in health food, for example—while sneaking off and doing the opposite—eating a bowl of ice cream on the sly. What contradictions come up for you as you are watching them, listening to them, writing down ideas from and about them?

Try to capture as much as you can about what it means to be human. Your assignment will call on you to interview someone quite different from yourself. If you are a Catholic, you might interview and profile an atheist. If you are a middle-class American, you might interview an international student. If you are a young person, you might interview someone your parents' age. The key here is to interview someone who does not share your values, who has a different way of thinking about life than you do. Try to get at this person's values and beliefs and why he or she holds them. Describe them as fully as you can for your audience.

feature 3.5

© MaxPhoto, 2009. Used under license from Shutterstock, Inc.

The Personal Essay and Concepts

Most of this chapter has been devoted to the idea of the personal essay as a form of expression. A final consideration here moves toward a concern with how personal experience can be used to expand on and explain a concept. This is a form that is often found in case study research in psychology fields, and it can also be a way of explaining interactions of the subjective and the conceptual.

One way to think about the personal is to consider that our subjectivities might not be only singular. One main aspect of ourselves may in fact only represent a small part of who we are. In fact, our personal lives might consist of commitments to different kinds of groups, and therefore, different discourses can help to explain and define our identities. Rather than one identity, say as a Catholic believer, we might also enjoy an identity as a musician, a collector of graphic novels, or an enthusiast of French cooking. Which of these subjectivities is most dominant? And should we allow ourselves to be defined by only one of them? Certainly, the question of who we are will be found in all of them. And exactly how that happens is worth the explanation.

Freshman writing instructor Kristy Hodson has designed an assignment meant to examine just this complexity, and she invites her students to explore their sense of self through varying discourses that define them. At the same time, she challenges some traditional genres with this assignment. Though engaged in the idea that our lives are written in by powerful social discourses, her students also write in personal terms that the academy sometimes does not accept. And yet the knowledge that is gained from writing and reading this work is as valid as the knowledge gained from a survey. Furthermore, consider the clarity that comes from the writing one of her students does in response to this question. The following essay by first year student, Katelyn Crombie, demonstrates how writing down the personal can clarify experiences for many.

Katelyn Crombie

Shuō Yīngyǔ!

Like most Americans, I am expected to only be one thing or another, to speak a certain way and to belong to "approved" discourse communities. Any deviance from the mainstream path is often met with a paraphrase of the common expression, "Speak English!" — as if using a unique voice changes my words into nonsense for my listeners. In her essay, "How To Tame a Wild Tongue," Gloria E. Anzaldúa asks for a "serpent's tongue" with which to express her differences while staying the same person. But would having those differences even matter if no one was able to understand them?

> "On houses and building tops,
> I swallow the beams and sundrops...
> I'll put on a diving tank
> And sing what I inhale." (Owl City)

My most misunderstood voice is my artist's voice. I have considered myself an artist since the first moment I picked up a pencil to draw, but I officially became recognized after I joined the online art community, DeviantART, and began taking actual art classes. And as such, I can say almost anything without people wondering whether or not I'm drugged up or otherwise crazy. For example: if someone knew I was an artist and I were to tell them not to cross a bridge because it is secretly a portal to another dimension and they'll find themselves on a path of floating glass stepping "stones" stretched across a vast expanse of purple stars over a sea of lava, the main things that would stand out would be my creativity and imagination — completely harmless albeit strangely timed. I can also use my artist's voice to explain deeper, often philosophical meanings behind certain things to people without coming off as pretentious, extremely intellectual, or "just faking it." I can change the obvious into the profound, the chaotic into something beautiful, and the simple observation into an enduring life lesson. If I wished, I could tell people that I feel "like the universe is collapsing in on itself, bit by bit, and life itself is hanging on a spider's thread" instead of just that I feel "really bad about life" at that particular moment. Therefore, I associate this discourse community not with other artists and their perspective tools and trades, but rather anything involving more than what's seen on the surface, thus making it a large and integrated part of my life. However, using this voice in everyday life is like talking in Elvish to English speakers. Even with a translator, a lot of the beauty and complexity involved is quickly lost or simplified too much to be effective. So how can I embrace my words when no one else knows what I'm saying?

> "Only question I ever thought was hard
> Was do I like Kirk or do I like Picard?" (Weird Al)

Another voice I have a difficult time with is my geeky voice. Most people don't know what a geek is, and tend to assume the term "geek" to be another word for a hipster, super-fan, or nerd who also likes technology. While the geek universe *does* overlap with certain fandoms and the nerd realm, it is much more complex than that. A non-geek who thinks they're a geek can usually quote a random *Star Wars* scene line-by-line before rattling off obscure facts about the production of George Lucas's creation, such as the techniques employed to make Yoda look like he was actually using the Force; and a nerd who acts like a geek may quote the same scene and explain the theories behind what the Force is and how Jedi are biologically able to use it. True "geek speak," however, could quickly evolve from a conversation about Yoda and his influence on the overall story to the ambiguity of his origins, the moral reasons behind his disagreements with Djinn Altis, the theoretical science behind building a lightsaber in real life, and other non-contributing details the *Star Wars* creative team had to figure out. While I am proud to use this voice around my friends because it lets me hold a deeper and more meaningful conversation with them, I find myself restricting it or smothering it altogether when around non-geeky fans or ordinary people. After all, what would it accomplish for me if I were to leave everyone else shaking their heads in confusion?

> "I wanted my children to have the best combination:
> American circumstances and Chinese character.
> How could I know these things do not mix?" (Amy Tan)

My last two voices are always intertwined, despite being complete opposites. Being born in China and adopted into an American family, I was technically a "clean slate" for the longest time. I could pick and choose between Chinese grace and American aggressiveness without being told that one was right and the other was wrong. My heritage was a bit of both cultures, as well as the emigrant Scottish culture on my dad's side, so celebrating Chinese New Year, Robert Burns' Day, and the 4th of July in the same year was not unusual for me. I could even reject parts of my heritage without being frowned upon. But as I've grown older, people focus more on their expectations of who I'm supposed to be, instead of who I am or who I want to become.

When I am around other Asians, I'm supposed to act like they do and like the things they like. I'm supposed to be sassy and fun, yet gentle at heart. I'm supposed to choose chow mein over hamburgers, anime over comic books, and one style of fashion over another. I find myself listening with my quiet Asian spirit, too embarrassed to give away the fact I'm a Chinese-born American, rather than American Chinese. I also pick up other characteristics, such as seeing all my desires as selfish, being embarrassed by actions otherwise acceptable to American culture, and exaggerating my politeness to strangers and my elders.

However, when I am around other Americans, I'm supposed to be who they are and like the things they like. I'm supposed to stand up for myself and be independent while having girlish tendencies for "cute" or "chic" things. I'm supposed to choose hot dogs over white rice, romantic adventure comedies over animated films, and the latest style of fashion over the casual look. I find myself pretending to be friendlier than I usually am, being too afraid to admit I'm no extrovert like those around me. I nod my head when people talk about pre-marital sex or "tolerance"/moral relativism or the latest in pop culture, swallow the tendency to buy into consumerism, and get mad at everyone else for "making this world worse off than it was before."

These voices did not clash before, and I resent society for forcing me into a mold that is not me. I don't want to be just one nationality at a time. I want to speak as I do with my family and closest friends, and not have to choose between one side and the other just because I am with a certain group. I want to be both kind and strong, quiet yet independent, morally and traditionally grounded yet willing to love others as they are. But if I were to speak with both voices at the same time, both cultures would point their fingers at me and claim betrayal; I am to be *gŏng hé* when around Asians (which would still put me at odds with my American side), and "gung-ho" when around Americans. Are the two truly irreconcilable?

I believe restoring the things lost in translation depends on how I speak to others, instead of whether or not I can speak with a "serpent's tongue." Yes, I can meld all my voices together, but if no one understands them then there is no point. I don't have to hold back who I am. I just need to remember interpretations must be made in "English" in order for people to truly appreciate me being an artist, geek, or Chinese American. I must also learn how to make the most impact while translating my thoughts; how else could I get people to wonder about having a hamburger and egg drop soup together, or why aliens seem to only visit Earth at night, or what it would be like if fish could fly and people could breathe underwater? The road to the mastery of "speaking English" will not be easy, but it will become the key to my future vocal freedom..

Works Cited

Al Yankovic. "White and Nerdy." *Straight Outta Lynwood.* Volcano, 2006. MP3 file.
Owl City. "Panda Bear." *Of June.* Universal Republic, 2010. MP3 file.
Tan, Amy. *The Joy Luck Club.* New York: G.P. Putman's Sons, 1989. Print.

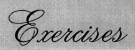

Exercise 1: Individual and Group Work

Jot down the first five ideas that come to your mind. Don't worry about form here. Just get them on paper. After you have done this, form groups of four. In your group, take turns sharing all five of your ideas. Your task as you do is to listen to how many of the ideas your group members share are like your own. Put a check mark in the margin by each idea of your own that others in your group have also come up with. After this, share your group's ideas with the whole class. As you listen to the other groups sharing their ideas, put more check marks by your five ideas that are similar to what others have shared.

In doing this exercise, you may come to understand how commonly shared your experiences are. Use that information to guide you in either 1) brainstorming more ideas, pushing yourself a little farther with your ideas, or 2) thinking about how you can make your idea stand out more, be really different from, and connect better with others as a commonly shared experience.

One important thing you might get from this is how many of your own ideas "off the top or your head," those ideas that first occur to you, are also the ideas that first occur to everyone else.

From the Other Angle: Deepening the Platitude or Commonplace

Exercise 2

To begin, jot down any ideas that come to you, any experiences or words or ideas, in response to the following sentences, but push yourself:

Doing the best you can is all relative to the crowd you want to please.
The crowd around me was all a little drunk anyway when I stood up.
You may know these details have been skipped, and I may know it too, but the people
we're with don't know it, and that's all that matters.
After that, I could go back to being bored.
All of a sudden, I realized that mom wasn't around. I was alone in the grocery aisle.

Works Cited

Carter, Michael. *Where Writing Begins: A Postmodern Reconstruction*. Carbondale: SIU Press, 2003.

Prelude and Fugue

I remember taking apart my saxophone as slowly as possible after the bell sounded, running the felt cloth through the body of the instrument to swab the spit that clung to its sides and pooled in the bottom. I was keenly aware of exactly how long it would take for the hallways outside to grow full and chaotic, perfect for me to merge into the hustle of my second life.

It is nearly impossible to be popular in middle school while at the same time being a devoted member of the band. Attempting the two endeavors is essentially counterproductive—an oxymoron. But somehow, for the last two years, I had managed to do this. I was first chair alto saxophone behind the doors of Mr. Hudson's band room and varsity track star everywhere else. And I preferred to keep the two worlds quite separate.

Although some might imagine that popularity just happens to a person, as if a mystical being much like the tooth fairy descends upon sleeping children and destines them to become popular, this idea could not be farther from the truth. At least in junior high, popularity is determined by which group an individual belongs to. There is no such thing as a popular girl. If she is popular, it is because she is "one of those popular girls." It is the same for boys.

At the beginning of the seventh grade, I was more than willing to accept their fragile friendship and a seat at their lunch table. Although it was just one table over from where I had previously sat, eating the same turkey sandwich and peeling off the iceberg lettuce, it felt like I had detached myself from mediocrity.

The thing that set us apart from the other girls was the laughter. It seemed we were always laughing about something hilarious, and the racket we created drew attention to us everywhere we went. Alyssa's laugh was the pride of the group. It was a kind of squawk that exploded from her mouth as her head jerked back and her eyes closed tightly. Our laughter served as proof that we were special and that our lives should be the envy of all.

At first, my job was simply to serve as another body standing in the exclusive "cool circle" that formed each morning outside of the school doors. And it was quite literally a circle. We stood shoulder to shoulder facing the center, gossiping, flirting, and keeping others out. I never spoke much, but no one noticed since the conversation went along fine without me.

By eighth grade, I had grown comfortable around these girls who laughed like hyenas and rotated through boyfriends with each other, sharing them like bags of popcorn. Once, during lunch, when we were all huddled in the bathroom checking our mascara and trying to pee daintily, I made a casual comment.

"Did you know that there is a right and wrong way to wear a belt?" I asked them as I stepped out of stall and started to wash my hands.

They were interested. "What do you mean?" one of the girls asked. She turned to face me and so did the others.

"Oh, I was just noticing that you have to go through the left belt loop first or else the design is upside down."

They all considered this for a moment and then simultaneously checked their own belt to make sure it was put on the proper way. In that moment as I watched them, I felt like the greatest authority on fashion. I had taught them something, and without question they had followed.

A few other instances of this nature occurred that same week and each time felt better than the last. I explained to them how combing wet hair was less damaging than brushing it—a beauty tip I had read in a magazine the night before. We had our moms drop us off at a local salon to purchase some combs together. I complained about the cruelty of having to be at school so early in the morning since girls our age needed at least nine hours of sleep at night. A few days later, a petition was being passed around about pushing back the school start time. I felt my status in the group shifting. I was no longer a useless accessory; I was its most precious gem.

In band class, I tried to maintain my new *queen bee* persona, but without my counterparts, it was a difficult task. I found myself under the spell of the classical motifs and bright fanfares, transported into the midst of a great battle or royal procession. The music played over and over in my head long after that hour in class, and I would catch myself humming a Sousa march as I twirled the combination on my locker or fed my pencil to the sharpener that hung on the wall. Even while I sat in my desk, my fingers would run through my part by memory, lightly tapping on the wood.

The way Mr. Hudson conducted would make anyone fall in love with music. Our eyes followed his hands through the air, and they seemed to dance independently on their own. When we came to the waltz section, his fingers would mimic the boom chuck chuck, boom chuck chuck of the percussion. He often compared music to the culinary arts saying that we must have a balanced sound like the perfectly centered platter that a waiter can hold with one hand.

He was tough too. Mr. Hudson demanded our best, and he let us know when we were falling short. I remember a few class periods that ended with him slamming his baton on the music stand and telling us that we had played "like crap." He told us we needed to practice and that we were wasting his time and the time of our classmates by making the same mistakes over and over again. "I hate conducting middle school bands," he would say, "so don't play like one."

One day after a long rehearsal, Mr. Hudson called me into his office. I was glad for the excuse to delay my entrance into the hallway a little longer.

"Lisa," he said, "I've been asked to select a student to play the National Anthem at the basketball tournament this weekend. Are you available?"

Mr. Hudson was glancing through papers on his desk as he spoke, unaware that I stood frozen in his doorway. The basketball tournament had been all we talked about for the last two weeks. Without realizing it, I had come to think of this coming weekend as my official commencement into my true place in society. The girls and I had painted T-shirts with the numbers of "our boys" on the backs. We had helped each other coordinate our hairstyles, shimmering blush bronzers, and lip-glosses so that somehow we each looked different while at the same time looking identical.

Yet, I was so mesmerized by Mr. Hudson's offer. Out of all his music students, he wanted me to play. I imagined myself standing in the middle of the gymnasium alone under the lights while the spectators surrounded me on all sides.

"Well, do you think you're up for it?" Mr. Hudson repeated. He swiveled in his chair to look at me.

I couldn't let him down. "Sure," I said, "That sounds great."

I wasn't sure how to tell the girls. Either way I knew that my stint with popularity would end the moment I put the word "band" into a sentence. Still, I thought of ways to introduce them to the other me: the secret, bona fide band nerd.

I might say, "Don't you just love the *Titanic* soundtrack? That composer is amazing."

Or perhaps I would try, "I have so much homework tonight." I would allow some time for them to agree with me and then slip it in subtly. "Yeah, and then I have to go to track practice and then play saxophone . . ."

When Saturday night came, I had still failed to prepare them for the shock. Instead, I prayed that they would all be in the bathroom at the same time or that two big men would start a fist fight right in front of them, and they would miss the performance all together.

I stepped onto the court and walked straight to the center, refusing to search for them in the crowd. After the announcer introduced me through the microphone, I planned to glue my eyes on the flag and forget that they were there. I wanted to play without picturing their awful faces, embarrassed that they had been so mistaken about me–realizing that I was only fool's gold in the end.

Then I heard the applause, and I was suddenly aware of how many people had been crowded into the gymnasium. I couldn't help it. I glanced up. A blur of people covered the bleachers on both sides and many stood or sat against the walls. They didn't seem particularly excited to hear a fourteen-year-old stutter her way through the National Anthem, but they clapped instinctively and turned to face the flag.

My hands quivered uncontrollably as I began, but then the long notes echoed off the ceiling, and those clear, reverberating pitches made my small body pulse with energy. I closed my eyes, and for the first time, I wasn't only playing the music; I was hearing it. For these few minutes, I forgot about their laughter, their clothes, and all of the other reasons I believed my life was full and good. Then the song was over.

Some say that we won't recognize the defining moments in our lives when they happen. We will simply look back in hindsight and see their significance in shaping who we are. But I think sometimes, right in the moment, you know that you are changing.

Grammar Interlude 3: Knowing a Phrase from a Clause

*****IMPORTANT DEFINITION*****

   *****NOTE: a phrase will be built around one part of speech, around a noun or a verb or an adjective or an adverb.

   A phrase is built around a noun or a verb, not both together. For example, "at the beach" is a phrase.

   A clause includes both a subject (noun or noun phrase) and a verb (or verb phrase). For example, "Bert ate the sundial" is a clause.

   Developing a Working Understanding of the difference between phrases and clauses leads to understanding two comma rules and the important concepts of coordination and subordination: a clause (independent or dependent) has both a subject (noun) and a verb; a phrase has either a noun or a verb, but not both.

   A clause can be independent **(IC)** (complete sentence) or dependent **(DC)** (incomplete/sentence fragment/modifies other)

For the following, (PP) = prepositional phrase, (NP) = noun phrase, and (VP) = verb phrase.

PHRASES and	CLAUSES
(PP) In the park	(IC) Sally isn't in the house.
(PP) Behind the refrigerator	(DC) When Burt stepped on the DVD player
(PP) After the show	(DC) After we left the show
(NP) The man	(IC) The man stood beside the priest
(PP) in the yellow convertible	(IC) What is the right answer?
(VP) was walking swiftly	

EX. 1. For the following, identify independent clause (ic), dependent clause (dc), or phrase (ph):

___ 1. Burt left the circus

___ 2. When Burt left the circus

___ 3. After leaving the circus

___ 4. "When in the course of human events . . ." (Let's bring this entire passage out and examine it)

___ 5. I will not raise taxes!

___ 6. When I am your president

___ 7. Read my lips

___ 8. Bert fed the ducks, and one of them followed him home

___ 9. At the day care center

___10. drank it slowly

EX. 2. In three passages from your own writing, put a brick around the main independent clause. Circle all prepositional phrases. Draw a squiggly line under all dependent clauses. These marked passages should be brought to class for workshop and presentation.

QUESTIONS FOR REFLECTION AND PRACTICE

What knowledge did you gain here?

Do these routines teach you anything of value for your own writing?

If so, what?

What will you do to connect with your future style and editing choices?

Chapter *Four*

Writing Arguments in Community

Chapter Overview

This chapter continues the focus on invention, though as seen from the perspective of ancient rhetoricians like Aristotle. Several concepts important to classical Rhetoric are introduced. The commonplace as a source for creating arguments is detailed. This view leads to a discussion of the social aspects of most writing and argument, especially the point that the ideas we come up with to support arguments must be persuasive to specific audiences. This is presented in a discussion of Burke's parlor. Following this, Aristotle's artistic proofs logos, ethos, and pathos are introduced, and finally we look at the structure that most arguments take.

Why People Might Resist Argument

Most people do not like to argue. They don't spend much time thinking about their positions on various issues, and they don't have files of facts or good reasons ready to support their ideas. Furthermore, they often note, arguing doesn't change peoples' minds or even cause them to rethink their positions. In fact, some people will say just about anything to defend their "side." This makes it seem worthless to get into debates, especially over political issues. After all, the world of politics is awash with corporate money. When big money controls the decisions of politicians, what is the point of debating anything?

To address this, consider the following scenario: A hybrid car sitting in a handicapped parking spot outside a shopping center. All three aspects of this—the new hybrid—and perhaps especially this is obvious if it gets ninety-five miles to the gallon—the parking spot it takes up, and the shopping mall have resulted from many extended arguments, some carried out in the realm of politics. In the case of the car, engineers drew up contrasting plans and argued for and against them, looking for the best possible car in those many plans. Arguments and dialogues ensued over issues perhaps only understandable to a few specialists. But these arguments needed to be heard and weighed before the best possible design for the car emerged. In all probability, the design did not simply emerge as a single drawing. It took more than one person's isolated inspiration. It took collaboration; people took sides and, for the sake of the end result, argued.

As for that handicapped parking space (assuming the hybrid owner has a handicapped parking sticker that makes this parking choice legal), it wouldn't have existed forty years ago—back when leaded gasoline was the norm and most cars got under twenty miles to the gallon. For that matter, neither would wheel chair ramps giving the physically handicapped access to public buildings. Those began to appear with increasing frequency after many debates over equal access, with many public arguments and senate hearings on the matter, until now public policy reflects our current "reality," which, if an alien visiting Earth didn't know better, might think has always been reality. Even so, I still come across road construction in my city where curbs are altered to make sidewalks wheel-chair accessible.

What has been said about hybrids and the rights of the disabled could be said of just about everything we accept as given now, from our current views on abortion and civil rights to the banning of cigarette ads on television. All are issues that people have debated to persuade others to what might be considered a more humane and enlightened public and civic culture. And they have often had to make their cases in city halls, state houses, and in the nation's capital. Absent City Hall or the State House, the same could even be said of our current views on the structure and purpose of the cosmos we inhabit—views that have over the last six hundred years seen many shifts and changes, as much the result of sustained arguments as discoveries. Though Galileo pointed his new telescope at Jupiter and reported that he had discovered moons circling around the giant planet, it took more than this evidence to replace the old, Aristotelian model of an Earth-centric universe with our current understanding. The change occurred gradually, with many arguments.

This is all to say, then, that arguments are always at the center of what is shaping our lives. In a culture that claims democratic principles, arguments inform civic and academic culture, and they have consequences. The places where this is not the case is in a tyranny, where argument is criminal and banned, or in a decadent culture where it is seen as trivial. Rome during the second century C.E. saw the toxic combination of both of these conditions, when public speaking became trivialized as mere performance, bringing on what has come to be known historically as a "second sophistic." In this public setting, where arguments were seen as entertainment on a par with a gladiator contest, public rhetoric had no social consequences and the Emperor could act as he pleased without any real public censure.

Today in the Culture Wars

In today's media-driven world, "talking heads" on television can appear to make parodies of argument; they seem as purposeless in this same way. This is certainly a reasonable observation when we begin to think about how big money, media, and corporate influence drive political campaigns and appear to influence what laws will be created and passed and, sometimes, even what news we will hear. Many people simply associate arguments with pointless contests or win-lose debates in which opponents attack one another's positions without listening to each other and resort to name-calling, slander, or charges of immorality. Many issues today, including gun regulation, abortion, gay marriage, the separation of church and state, the role of government in our lives, stem cell research, funding for Medicare and Social Security, and global warming all represent important, ongoing, complex debates that drive deep divisions and have resulted in unresolvable differences. The positions that we take on many of these debates—gay marriage, abortion, the role of government and religion in our lives, to name a few of them—are so deeply intertwined with our values that they have come to represent aspects in a larger conflict we sometimes flippantly refer to as the culture wars.

This metaphor of a culture at war refers to arguments that engage people from different political parties and philosophies, especially people who take a progressive, liberal view and people who see themselves as conservatives. Though occasional agreements are reached over side issues, the larger differences over the issues are rooted in civic, moral, and religious assumptions that are not always open to reason, and so minds and positions are not changed overnight. Because most of us have longstanding views based in more than passing feelings, our views will have some unexamined elements, and arguments will seem to fall on deaf ears, just when it seems that reasoned argument is most called for. But instead, emotional appeals, slogans, and name calling, usually with God and devil terms* make our favorites seem like heroes of our values and our opponents evil caricatures of everything we hate.

The divisions that constitute American culture wars have appeared over many different periods and have involved various arguments. Perhaps one period that is often cited among journalists can be seen in the Scopes Trial of the 1920s, when a biology teacher at a school in the Deep South was put on trial for teaching evolution in his class. Perhaps it is safe to say that one specific area where American culture wars are evident is in the area where science and religious belief conflict. Schools in some districts in Texas and the South still see court cases that centered on this issue, though now the cases concern the legality of teaching Creationism as a scientific perspective in the public schools.

The 1930s saw the creation of the New Deal and the passage of Social Security. New Deal programs also led to the rise of opposition views to fight them, with progressives and conservatives arguing over issues that are still seen today.

God Terms, Devil Terms

Richard Weaver notes the use of God terms and devil terms, for approval and censure, as value-laden words that come to stand for what a culture at a certain time does or does not value. For example, he notes that "progressive" and "science" came in the 1950s to be God terms, terms of approval, while the word "Nazi," a devil term during the second world war, was quickly replaced by the terms "communist" and "un-American" as devil terms of the 1950s. So also, more recently, President George W. Bush was often called a "Nazi" by opponents, and President Barrack Obama was often censured as a "socialist," a devil term among conservatives. The suggestion when thinking about this is as follows: hearing these terms, we can see what people do and do not value; and we can notice that complexity is being reduced to the simple "either/or" dualism of the cartoon.

Behind many recent campaigns on Social Security, for example, one hears language being given to support or go against growth in government programs, over new funding for what is, in essence, a New Deal program, and programs like Medicare. The debate seems to center on how government should function in our lives. Should government help make peoples' lives better? Should it help the economy and support new businesses? Or should it simply stay out of the way? And how much of our taxes should be used to encourage government programs?

The passage of *Roe v. Wade* in 1973 leading to legalized abortions also resulted in a wave of reaction, with groups like the Moral Majority taking shape in conservative and Evangelical religious denominations and becoming influences on the Republican party.

As can be seen, arguments over these issues and their framing continue to find audiences and concern, because the issues are not resolved for all concerned.

Another ongoing debate that stands in contrast to those above involve gun control debates that are not necessarily carried out between liberals and conservatives in the way abortion is. In these debates, both Democrats and Republicans claim their identity as card-carrying members of the NRA and take pains to show that they understand the need for guns. Nevertheless, the need for new gun control legislation remains a complicated issue that has caused deep divisions. At the center of debate is a concern with how the Second Amendment to the U.S. Constitution should be interpreted in light of gun ownership. Indeed, because it involves reading and interpreting the Constitution, it might be related to the larger culture wars in American society. Arguments seem to lead to greater divisions, and the debates flare up every time gun violence in a school or university makes headlines. The arguments are predictable in the way they seem to fall along familiar fault lines, with some using slogans like "Guns don't kill people; people do," and arguing that we live in a violent culture that is fostered by Hollywood and video game creators. Others argue for stricter gun laws, or more strict enforcement of background checks for purchasers of firearms. But few seem to be arguing for an end to gun ownership or abolishing the Second Amendment.

Though divisive arguments over gun control may never be resolved through appeals to reason, they are worth having, and they are worth writing about. Though we might not solve all conflicts for all parties concerned, engaging the argument leads to learning more about the issues.

Reasons for Argument

Certainly, many arguments can be settled by appeals to reason. Many issues concerned with diet, body image, and lifestyle fit this category, as do other issues of public health, unless, of course, it involves abortion or stem cell research. And not all arguments are as deeply imbedded in conflicting values that seem irreconcilable as those concerned with the right to life or the rights of gun owners.

In all academic departments, arguments are made over issues that concern other professionals in the discipline. In the field of English, scholars may argue that Shakespeare's Hamlet is not a melancholy prince who can't make up his mind, but a reasonable man who delays killing his uncle until he has more evidence of the man's guilt beyond the word of a ghost. Writing teachers debate the usefulness of peer group editing, and they gain adherents to their views based on their classroom, anecdotal evidence, and student testimonies.

As is represented in most universities and colleges, early rhetoric and early philosophy were taught as the best way to learn to live, and people learned how to argue. The best philosophies, positions, and policies for action came about through peoples' sustained debates as they tested opinions in the effort to find what was the best possible opinion. Behind every good and fair proposal to shape a fair society, there have been many arguments. And when we argue, perhaps we are trying to figure out for ourselves what the best course of action is for us to take. We argue to persuade others, certainly, but we also argue to persuade ourselves, to hear the best possible views. We argue to discover.

This may seem an ideal when considered in light of the way Hollywood and TV present arguments. But it is the reason to value argument for the way it can help to clarify issues. Consider the following essay written by a student, Dalia Velasco.

Dalia Velasco

Crime Shows on Television

Lights, camera, action! The scene opens with a suspicious male entering the back door of a Utah home in the late hours of the night. Moments later we see him walking out the back door; only this time he is carrying a vague figure in his arms. The scene then moves to a mother awakening in the morning to find her home broken into and her six-year-old daughter missing, nowhere to be found. Immediately she phones the police to report her missing child. Within hours of searching, the body of a lifeless six-year-old girl is found lying cold in a nearby canal. It is later discovered that the child was not only murdered but forcefully raped. Unfortunately, this story was not a murder by the book. On June 26, 2012 Terry Lee Black, who was no stranger to Utah law enforcement, kidnapped, raped, and murdered Sierra Newbold and proceeded to dump her body in the West Jordan canal (Carlisle). Sadly, this story line is also encountered in many thrill-seeking crime shows such as *CSI, Forensic Files, Snapped,* and *America's Most Wanted.* As crime scene investigation television shows are becoming increasingly popular with general audiences, producers are sending the wrong message to viewers, negatively affecting their view on crime scene investigation.

Crime scene investigation shows have increased in popularity among audiences, and at almost any time of the day one is likely to find a showing. These programs have been largely accepted among all audiences as sound entertainment that enlightens us in the forensic and legal careers that they display. Neal Gabler, in *Life the Movie: How Entertainment Conquered Reality,* explains that "after decades of public-relations contrivances and media hype, [...] life has become art, so that the two are now indistinguishable from each other." Unfortunately this same concept, after years of media coverage, has trickled into our legal system and shifted the ideas of jurors who have a great responsibility in court rooms. Overall, it has changed societies view on the process of investigation and prosecution, and is changing the way protocol is supposed to function in the legal court system.

There is no denying that crime investigation shows are exaggerated for entertainment rather than to portray accurate and honest coverage, but too often audience members interpret what they watch as real. Crime scene shows "[fall] somewhere between crime dramas and reality shows" due to the exaggerated plots that include dramatic music inserts and special effects (Kort-Butler). These shows often spotlight such interesting story lines behind the crimes that the viewer forgets it is about a terrible crime. Although these shows are meant to represent real life events, they embellish the reality of the situation to better fit the theatrical script. Crime scene investigation shows also portray investigators as heroes, because they are the ones searching, analyzing, and processing

evidence, when in actuality there are numerous individuals involved throughout the investigation of a crime. Each profession in the team effort to solve the
crime is individually demanding, each involving, "their own education, training,
and methods" which in no way could all be accomplished by one lone detective (Houck). Through these shows viewers are given the best of both worlds
because in the end, good always perseveres, still allowing the audience to be
tantalized by their dark side (Barney). But, when referring back to the story of
the six-year-old girl who was kidnapped, raped, and murdered, it is difficult to
believe that viewers find the variety of situations intriguing, and even as a form
of entertainment.

One of the main misconceptions individuals have is they watch crime scene
programs as a glamorous and exciting occupation, but do not realize the amount
of science and work that this involves. In recent years, the forensics field has
become popular with younger generations, largely in part to crime investigation
shows on television. When viewing these shows, younger individuals are captivated by the glory of being involved in such a heroic and action-packed job, due
to Hollywood's depiction of it. These shows have led to "increasing enrollments in
science courses at high schools and universities" (Turnbull). Although students
enrolling in science classes for the field is reasonable, the disappointment they
often feel after realizing what the forensics field actually consists of is inconve-
nient. Many watch these shows and believe it to be very lively, constantly making
new discoveries to solve the case. In actuality, most labs do not have the kind
of technology that crime scene shows present because, "scientific labs that are
featured on the shows are also nothing but fancy Hollywood sets. There are very
few law enforcement agencies in the nation that have the technologies as seen on
those shows" (Stranger). Often the gadgets used on shows are not real inventions,
but make-believe gadgets made fit the story line. According to the article, "Fed:
Glamorous Crime Shows Affecting Real Life Forensics," they are also placing a lot
of pressure on the forensic field to, "examine every piece of evidence," and to have
a, "complete [investigation] in quickly." These expectations are not realistic for
the forensic community, because most times these scientists have multiple cases
at one time and cannot afford to place all their time and attention on one single
case. Most of the time such far-fetched efforts are not required for the investigators
to make what should be a solid case.

To further deepen the problem, the effects of crime shows have reached
our legal court room jurors, who have impracticable expectations for the court
system. With crime programs being so popular, many jurors have become accus-
tomed to the entertainment factor of the legal system displayed on television;
and in turn they bring that to the court room with them. According to the article, "TV Crime Dramas Skew Perception of System," people who regularly watch
crime scene investigation shows are "more likely than nonviewers to have a
distorted perception of the U.S. criminal justice system." They tend to see the
courtroom as Hollywood drama implementing that certain "wow-factor," and in

order for it to be true, there must be a substantial amount of evidence that is brought forward. It has even been found that if the defendant is convicted as guilty and does not confess soon after, then jurors doubt if the defendant was ever truly guilty. Among this, evidence must be concrete and scientifically based like DNA, fabric, and residue samples, even if it is not needed for the case. A judge noted that these shows have taught the jurors about DNA tests, but not when to use them (Houck). Another aspect that has been affected is the trust of evidence and the amount of work that has been put into it, making jurors more susceptible to believing that the evidence being presented in the court room is automatically true. Kimberlianne Podlas, a media law professor, stated that, "the [shows] actually may help prosecutors because jurors assume the evidence presented is a result of an exhaustive investigation" (Booth). This could be detrimental to a case and the defendant, due to the lack of critical thinking over the evidence being presented in the courtroom.

Some say that crime investigation programs have educational value. The article "Fed: Glamorous Crime Shows Affecting Real Life Forensics," points out that these television shows have, "a positive educational value." However, these shows are teaching the average person how to commit crimes that they may not have ever thought about. In past years, it has been found, "rapists are becoming more sophisticated when committing sex crimes, leaving less evidence in their wake" (Dutton). By making viewers increasingly aware of forensic technology, it allows them to find loopholes in order to dodge the consequences of their criminal acts. It was reported that a rape victim testified that after she was raped the assailant, "forced [her] to shower after the attack to wash off any evidence"; this unfortunately demonstrates the possibility that criminals are becoming more sophisticated (Goehner). In audiences that are not committing crimes, it causes unnecessary fear to some rare cases, causing individuals to become paranoid about situations that are very rare. It could even go to the extent that it normalizes the thought of murder in our society. In reality not many people are ever directly affected by a tragic murder or crime, but when they do occur, rarely do they play out like they are depicted on television.

One may say that criminals are probably not learning their techniques and skills from a television show. Detective Doering would agree, by saying, "criminals learn evasive techniques through the prison system [more] than they do watching TV" (Stranger). Although this is partly true, some criminals could watch crime investigation shows as a plug into the other end of the spectrum in order to learn techniques to cover his trails efficiently. The main concept that criminals could learn from crime investigation programs are the evidence and features that investigators search for. Criminals are not necessarily senseless people, and given the chance they are likely to accept information that may allow them to successfully commit crimes and get away with it.

Clearly, the airing of crime scene investigation shows is more damaging to society than beneficial. Crime investigation shows incorrectly influence television viewers to observe certain situations in the wrong lighting, normalizing the thought of murder and theatrics of the courtroom. They also give audience members untrue ideas about the career, and enlighten them about concepts once foreign to them. Forensics is based on science rather than heroism, and many cases that should have been guilty go dismissed because of the false ideas many people seem to cling to.

Works Cited

Barney, Chuck. "Investigating TV Crime shows' Success; Procedurals are Popular among Viewers. For some it's the Story, for Others it's the Characters." *Los Angeles Times:* D.28. Dec 25 2009. *Los Angeles Times.* Web. 7 Nov. 2012.

Booth, Brittney. "Crime shows Seeping into Jury Selections." Knight Ridder/Tribune Business News: 1. May 09 2006. ABI/INFORM Complete. Web. 7 Nov. 2012.

Carlisle, Nate. "Suspect in Custody for Killing Utah Girl Sierra Newbold." Utah Local News - Salt Lake City News, Sports, Archive - *The Salt Lake Tribune.* N.p., 10 July 2012. Web. 6 Nov. 2012. <http://www.sltrib.com/sltrib/news/54462742-78/newbold-girl-sierra-murder.html.csp>.

Dutton, Audrey. "More Rape Cases Go Unsolved: Police and Experts Put Part of the Blame on Crime shows, which can Provide Clues on Covering One's Tracks." McClatchy - *Tribune Business News:* 1. Sep 19 2006. ABI/INFORM Complete. Web. 7 Nov. 2012.

"Fed: Glamorous Crime Shows Affecting Real Life Forensics." AAP General News Wire: 1. Jun 14 2005. ProQuest Research Library. Web. 7 Nov. 2012 .

Gabler, Neal. *Life the Movie: How Entertainment Conquered Reality.* New York: Knopf, 1998. Print.

Goehner, Amy Lennard, Lina Lofaro, and Kate Novack. "Where CSI Meets Real Law And Order." *Time* 164.19 (2004): 69. Academic Search Premier. Web. 7 Nov. 2012.

Houck, Max M. "CSI: Reality." *Scientific American* 295.1 (2006): 84-89. Academic Search Premier. Web. 6 Nov. 2012.

Kort-Butler, Lisa A., and Kelley J. Sittner Hartshorn. "Watching The Detectives: Crime Programming, Fear of Crime, And Attitudes About The Criminal Justice System." *Sociological Quarterly* 52.1 (2011): 36-55. Academic Search Premier. Web. 6 Nov. 2012.

Stranger, Emily. "For Real Police, Crime shows on TV are a Bust." McClatchy - *Tribune Business News,* Aug 04 2008. ABI/INFORM Complete. Web. 7 Nov. 2012.

Turnbull, Sue. "Crime As Entertainment: The Case of the TV Crime Drama." *Continuum: Journal of Media & Cultural Studies* 24.6 (2010): 819-827. Academic Search Premier. Web. 6 Nov. 2012.

"TV Crime Dramas Skew Perception of System." *USA Today Magazine* 138.2775 (2009): 11-12. Academic Search Premier. Web. 7 Nov. 2012.

Details of Argument: Thesis, Opposing Views, and Supporting Evidence

Most arguments are made of at least three elements: A focused thesis; a consideration and refutation of the most reasonable claims of opposing arguments; and a chain of well-presented reasons supporting the main claim of the argument. We will take them in this order.

Element 1: An Arguable Thesis

This first element seems nothing new or different from the five paragraph theme. And yet it is. The thesis of the five paragraph theme is an expository statement that stresses three random points about a general topic. And the statement is one of purpose, as in "In this essay I will explain..." None of this helps with writing an argument. An argument is not a collection of three random ideas you happened to think up in a short period of time but a specific chain of reasoning carefully considered and persuasively given. The thesis for an argument will not carry that statement of intention ("In this essay I will argue..."), and it will not need to state what every paragraph in the essay is about; instead, it will give the main claim or idea being supported by every aspect of the essay. It is, in effect, the argument in a sentence or two.

An arguable thesis usually reflects our best, narrowed thinking about an issue of some controversy. The word itself, thesis, actually once involved for some ancient writers the asking of a question, and this suggests thinking being done before a final position is announced. Consider, for example, the explanations for the exercise known as "thesis" as found in two writers, the Roman teacher Quintillian and Theon. Both saw the matter of the thesis as concerned first with a general question—for example, should one marry? Quintillian wrote that a question like this could then be applied to specific circumstances, as in "Should Cato marry?" The point of a question like this, however, which was explained in Theon, seemed to be that the thesis was concerned with a "question that is in doubt" (Kennedy 87).

Today, we no longer see the thesis in this way, as "a question that is in doubt." We prefer to think of it as an assertion that is settled and something to hang onto and to prove. Thus, the matter of the thesis is seen as the chief goal of "pre-writing," as something to find the proper wording for so it can be asserted as settled. The problem today is essentially represented as involving making sure that the thesis is narrowed. In contrast, Quintillain tells us that the thesis was a matter of a question, or a quest: the examples, found in both Quintillian and in Theon, include the general and specific forms, as in "Should one marry?" The difference is obvious. In the ancient program, we have a question and a method for exploring it. Today, the matter is already settled. What can be learned from the ancient writers on this question, however, has to do with our approach to process and our interest in generating the best possible thesis. And this comes through the asking of good questions that we seek to answer.

Thesis as Question: **Before Formulating Your Position**

Set up an imaginary debate between two to four participants and ask/raise questions about an area of argument or concern. Is marriage the best way for a society to raise its youth? Should education be privatized? Should same-sex partners be given the right to marry?

In your preliminary exploration, allow various sides of the debate to be expressed and heard, and use this preliminary exploration to guide you as you formulate a clear thesis that can be argued.

Thesis Statements

One valuable lesson that will emerge from writing the five-paragraph theme and then going beyond it is the sense that the essay you write will need a thesis statement, also known as a main point, or, in the vernacular, an answer to the reader's question of "So what?" or "Why should I care?"

A good thesis idea will capture the essence or main argument of your essay. It can be controversial or declarative. Most important, however, is that it will guide your essay and reader, preventing her from asking the deadly question, "So what?" A good thesis will keep her reading. As long as the main argument of the essay is clear, it is possible that the thesis won't even appear in the essay as an actual statement. But the reader will be able to say, "This writer is against gun control." But not having the thesis appear in the essay is not the same as saying that the thesis can be broad or unclear. The following are examples of bad attempts to convey a thesis.

A Thesis Is Never a Question

Should we outlaw handguns? Should the gun shows in Texas where Mexican Cartels are getting weapons be banned? Should all students be required to take music classes in junior high school? Was Hemingway a good novelist? These questions are not the correct form for a thesis, but they are worth asking if you are unsure of your position and want to learn more. If that is the case, you are in the invention stage and wanting to figure out a way to invent your arguments. Asking the question and then jotting down arguments for all sides will help you to develop your ideas. From this, you can arrive at a clear sense of your position and what you want to argue when you write your paper.

A Thesis Is Never a Phrase or Dependent Clause

Whether to outlaw handguns. Taking music lessons in middle school, Hemingway as a novelist—in each of these cases, no clear position is spelled out.

Examples of Good Thesis Statements

In contrast, consider the following.

1. We should outlaw handguns. They are too easy to conceal.
2. The gun shows in Texas should require serious regulation, with the background of every buyer heavily scrutinized.
3. Music should be a part of every middle school curriculum for every student. If needed, take the money from sports programs to support music.
4. Ernest Hemingway was a better short story writer than a novelist.

With each of these, we know where the writer stands. And though we might disagree with them, we might think about how a writer would go about organizing an essay in such a way that they might prove or support each.

Element 2: Considering and Conceding to or Refuting Opposing Views

Second, it is important to any argument to give some space to relevant and reasonable, or at least popular, opposing arguments. We do this, not to show that we agree with the opposition, but to show that we are aware of them, have done our homework, and have an answer for them. If, for example, I want to argue for stricter laws regarding background checks for the purchase of firearms, I will probably have to raise the opposition slogan—simply because it is popularly believed—that "when guns are outlawed, only outlaws have guns." I will want to raise this early in my essay, right after my introduction, and then show what is wrong with it and why, for example, this doesn't apply to background checks, which will prevent gangs and the criminally insane from buying weapons.

This aspect of argument, it should be noted, is the least understood and practiced among new writers. Perhaps this is the case because we are too used to thinking of writing only in terms of information, which doesn't require mentioning opposing arguments. Or we are used to hearing only the persuasion of advertising, where to mention a competitor is to give them free air time.

Whatever the reason, this second element of argument is often overlooked by writers new to debate. They will see this concept of considering ideas of an opposition view as a sign of weakness. Like parents who present a united front to their children, they believe that they need to ignore any voices of dissent that might undermine their parental authority. Like a television commercial, we believe we should drone on about only the benefits of our product.

The problem is that we are not being parents when we argue. Nor are we selling people on a product. We are working with ideas, and ideas should be tested. And contrary to the commonplace idea, the truth is that with a college-level audience, if we do not anticipate possible objections to our thesis, the chances are very high that our audience, used to opposing discourses, will do it for us. And if we haven't shown that we've considered these views and rejected them, then we won't long have an audience for our ideas. If, for example, I were to argue that "guns don't kill people, people do" without considering why gun control advocates are not persuaded by this idea, then they won't find my slogan persuasive. Instead, they will dismiss my argument as the work of someone who hasn't really thought in any depth about the issues.

It is important, then, to consider relevant and reasonable opposing views, because it makes our argument appear that much more reasonable.

Element 3: Support and Evidence for the Claim

After giving opposing views their place in our reasoning so that we have successfully shown either that these views do not have merit or that some of them are of some limited value—we give the opposition certain reasonable concessions—then we provide our reasons for our argument. Placing the support for our position at the end means that we are giving our reasons for our views when they will be most listened to.

The kind of evidence we find we need to make in support of our claims will usually require more than just three random reasons given in a five paragraph theme. Instead, different kinds of evidence or proofs will need to be raised, depending on our subject and the values our audience holds, and that means going beyond mere citing of statistics. We might believe that any set of statistics will make us convincing and persuasive in our argument about gun laws, for example, but statistics may not win over an audience that believes that in politics there are "lies, damned lies, and statistics," as Mark Twain once quoted

Benjamin Disraeli as saying. If an audience is convinced that repealing the Second Amendment of the Constitution is an act leading to tyranny, all bills to ban weapons will be seen as wrong-headed infringements on basic rights. We will certainly use statistics, but we will also need to reason with our audience. To be persuasive, we need to know the people we are persuading. This does not mean merely assuming we know what they believe, but finding out.

Most arguments are built on three kinds of proofs, *ethos*, *pathos*, and *logos*. Though Aristotle stressed in his writing the importance of reason to argument, he was very clear that all kinds of proof have their place. And some recent researchers have noticed that the most persuasive appeals are those that, like analogy and the use of examples, help a writer to demonstrate a problem or a given set of reasons. It should also be noted that *logos*, *ethos*, and *pathos* do not represent a list of rules that must always be followed. These are simply general categories of kinds of proof, used when most people argue, and their support usually involves all three kinds of proof.

Logos, the *enthymeme*, and Audience

Logos is usually defined as the appeal to reason. It involves elements of an argument that appeal to our best thinking and might include cause-effect reasoning, or reasoning from a basic, agreed upon premise. It might involve an extended analogy or a demonstration of the reasonableness of something more than it involves the simple use of statistics. In fact, in many cases, statistics are easily dismissed as outdated, manipulated, or not relevant to a particular case, as easily as an appeal to authority or quoting someone important on an issue. The slogans one reads on social networking sites attributed to Albert Einstein, Abraham Lincoln, Mother Theresa, or Martin Luther King, Jr. might preach well to those who already agree with their ideas. But they won't persuade anyone who already has good reasons to think differently.

Most reasoning, certainly, is either deductive—arguing from a major premise that is held to be true—or inductive—drawing conclusions from a large sampling of evidence. Deduction was traditionally the realm of philosophy and theology, where reasoning followed from general statements that were accepted as true. Induction has formed the basis for scientific thinking, with reasoning based on careful collection of data and observation of experience. Both deduction and induction are often used in combination in argument.

In philosophy courses, we often encounter the syllogism, a three statement pattern of reasoning. The most famous example is this one:

"All men (and women) are mortal.

Socrates was a man.

Therefore, Socrates was a mortal."

In this syllogism, the first statement, called the major premise, sets out two categories—all men and how they are all mortal. The second statement, called the minor premise, places a particular example or man in the first category of men, which then helps us to locate him in the third statement, called the conclusion, in the category of all mortals. This deductive formula is rigid in its form and leads to conclusions that, if we accept the major premise/first statement as true, are irrefutable and persuasive.

Given the force of deduction, many thinkers search for "first statements" or principles on which to base their thinking, convinced that if their reader can see the reasonableness of the first statement, then the conclusion must be agreed upon by all who are reasonable. Perhaps the most famous example of an argument based on deduction is the American Declaration of Independence, a most controversial document that led to a most controversial war.

The syllogism on which the Declaration is based goes something like this:
"Governments that infringe on the rights of the governed must be resisted.
The British Monarchy has infringed on the rights of the colonies.
Therefore, the colonies must resist and abolish ties with the throne of England."

We should add to this the general belief of a democracy that government exists to protect and establish the rights of the governed. And in the Declaration of Independence, it is the middle term, the minor premise, that is given great detail, amounting to a list of grievances against the English king, attempting to prove legally that he was in fact trampling upon the basic rights of the colonists.

But the first premise, that governments that restrict and trample on the rights of the governed need not be obeyed and, in fact, should be resisted, is not the absolute truth that people in a democracy might think it is. In its day, the leaders of the American rebellion/revolution knew that they were striking out into controversy and would be executed if they were defeated.

Finding first principles that are uncontroversial in all cases is the struggle with deduction, and many writers find it more expedient in most arguments, since they are not writing a declaration, to not spell out all terms of their deduction. Instead, they may leave the major or minor premise unstated and implicit, easily recognized by the reader but not made emphatic. When writers and speakers do this, they are using what is called the rhetorical syllogism, or *enthymeme*, which is typically captured in a single statement. The *enthymeme* can run something like this: "As a new governor, Sally will solve our economic troubles because she has been a successful businesswoman." In this *enthymeme*, the unstated major premise is this: "All successful business women will be fiscally effective governors."

In several recent elections, one in California, and even a recent presidential race, this argument was made, though unsuccessfully. In most cases, though we might believe this statement to be true, it is actually more of a commonplace, and idea that many people have come to accept as true. It is probably true that the person making the claim knows how to keep a budget, but the statement that good business people make fiscally responsible governors or senators or presidents can be challenged simply by looking at the differences between people in business and people holding offices: in most cases, people run businesses and have power over decisions. They can make decisions that are immediately carried out. In contrast, most politicians must, given the very nature of democracy, work through compromise. When they send a bill to the legislature, they must also try to win supporters to their bill. What for the business leader is a unilateral decision is in politics a wish to be carried out that often is not. The politicians who make the claim that they know how to clean up the economy are hoping that we will accept that they will be able to do so through the force of their personality—and this falls under *ethos*.

Other *enthymemes* include the one discussed in Feature 4.1 in this chapter, that television and other social media have shortened our attention span. It might include the following as well: "Without love, no marriage will work." At face value, most Americans hold to the premise that marriage must be based on love. But for centuries, in many countries, marriage was based on arrangements between families. If one were to challenge the American idea, one need only point to the high divorce rate in this country in contrast to the divorce rate in other countries. Furthermore, most people who accept the idea that love is the basis of marriage also agree with the commonplace that if a person "falls out of love," then he or she no longer needs to stay in the marriage. The "loveless marriage" makes the stuff of many movies.

The point is not to marry without love, however, but to notice what happens when we use reason in argument. The most common feature of *logos* is the rhetorical syllogism, or the *enthymeme*, and in each of the cases given here, it allows us to focus on the reasoning being used and to see both its persuasiveness with certain audiences and its limits. When we understand that another person is basing an argument for more restrictions on teachers to make them more effective, we can note the need for families to support teachers more, and that a strong determiner on a child's success in school is not just the teacher, but also the positive involvement of the parents.

In each case, the *enthymeme* makes clear the basis of our reasoning, and in each case, since we are dealing with commonplaces and not absolute truths, we can challenge that basis. Or, our audience will agree with it and be persuaded by it.

Ethos and Pathos

Ethos is the appeal of a good character. It is expressed through word choice, through reasoning, and through the sincere expression of good will. In many cases, it is hard to pin down in an argument, though it comes up, for example, when a writer mentions being a doctor in an argument about a health care issue. *Ethos* involves our credibility and even authority, our ability to show audiences and readers our commonness with them, our ability to side with their situation. The appeal of a good character is often seen as the main persuasive appeal, which is why we often see celebrities getting out and using their fame to stump for issues that matter to them.

Pathos is the appeal to emotions, an appeal that can be used to manipulate people or to put a human face on a problem like sex trafficking or gun violence. The well-known problem with this appeal is that it is easily misused, but an effective use of *pathos* can serve to illustrate or demonstrate a problem and how it affects people, and this is persuasive. A good introduction to a controversial topic can often be the introduction of a particular incident in which a real person was affected by some aspect of the issue we wish to argue for or against. Doing this involves us. We do need to keep in mind, of course, that one case like this is an anecdote, and not proof of anything.

On the Commonplace and Resisting Reductive Thinking

We have begun to describe the main elements of argument, though to discuss only these elements is to be too reductive. To write a successful argument, we must follow the lead of the second requirement in considering opposition viewpoints: we need to consider our audience. Argument always occurs in community, not in isolation. And it involves logic, but it also involves values and beliefs. When thinking about these elements of argument—about thesis, opposing views, and what Aristotle called the three "artistic proofs"—we need to be aware of how each of them is reflected in how we think about audience.

One of the most common aspects of audience we should consider in more depth involves the part of community thinking that functions in the use of the *enthymeme* as a form of logos, or reason, as the place of values. Usually based, as noted above, in "commonplaces," these general statements of how people and the world in general work might also be seen in most peoples' thinking. In creative writing, commonplaces are seen as tendencies in word or thought to avoid. But when we are debating, it pays to listen to the ideas that people claim are true without giving much evidence for them. Commonplaces, like the commonplace given in Writing Prompt 4 of this chapter, involve people and their experiences. They often appear as truisms or maxims. "Best friends make good marriage partners," one might argue. "Children who grow up without siblings are spoiled," another might say, or "It's not what you say but how you say it." These are statements sometimes backed up by our experiences, but they are passed off as generalizations that may or may not actually be true. Evidence to the contrary can exist in each case.

feature 4.1   Writing Prompt 4

Aristotle's Answer (Indirectly) to the Question of Shortened Attention Spans

The argument has circulated for some time that too much television viewing reduces viewers' attention spans. By taking in programming interrupted every ten minutes for advertising, or so the argument goes, we have become habituated to resting our minds after little effort. We can't pay attention for very long. This state of affairs has affected the way we are able to take in information. Perhaps most sadly, some suspect, it has resulted in impoverished political discourse. When viewers can't handle complexity, politicians don't have to explain themselves very clearly. They can get away with not having to talk about their policies and instead run negative political campaigns in which they portray their opponents as "socialists," "right-wingers," "cowboys," "friends of terrorists," or whatever "devil terms" are enjoying cultural currency.

In the fourth century BCE, Aristotle noted something similar about people's attention spans when attending to a speech, though TV was nowhere to be seen. Most people were not trained in concentration, and it was Aristotle's view that people could only listen to so much in a speech and still follow it. For this reason, he noticed, the most effective public speakers tended to rely on shortened syllogisms, or chains of reasoning, which drew on what he referred to as commonplaces and opinions, sources of reason where groups of people found agreement and shared assumptions (42). These commonplaces might or might not have much empirical evidence behind them, but they were found by most members of a culture to be persuasive and intuitively correct. One example of a commonplace found today, certainly, is the notion this blog begins with, that watching television shortens one's attention span. Again, this is a statement that may or may not be true, and it may or may not be supported by empirical studies. The important part is that it is recognizable as an intuitively correct possibility, which then encourages social assent. And, of course, it can be either confirmed or contested. That is, it can itself be debated.

The Commonplace as a Source of Argument

Some might include the following: "To get ahead in society, you need to know the right people," or a variation on this theme, which might go something like this: "It's not what you know (in other words, don't bother getting a college education or advanced degree) but who you know." Yet another commonplace, which has resulted, incidentally, in a number of federal programs, might run something like this: "Young people today can't read or write. Literacy skills in the public schools are clearly in decline." Again, these are not ideas that are proved by "evidence." The evidence behind them usually winds up being experience.

Commonplaces, as general statements about how the world works, are always persuasive to particular, specific audiences. For example, largely white, middle-class audiences may have trouble believing that the local police occasionally may engage in racial profiling. They may even ignore evidence of such behaviors. But even so, commonplaces can usually be refuted or challenged or upheld with new evidence. For example, recent studies in cognition and brain research have born out Aristotle's observations about an audience's ability to stay with complicated reasoning. One researcher (Kellogg) notes the evidence that we are simply not able to store a great deal of information in short-term memory. Certainly it is possible to train ourselves, to increase our attention spans, and to hold more than one idea in our brains at a time. But for the average listener and reader, those who are not trained, short-term memory will limit both how well we retain information we've read or heard and how well we are able to write. It will certainly contribute to how well we follow the complicated parts of a public speech. A limited short-term memory is also one very good reason why writing teachers often stress invention strategies and writing thoughts down in a sketchy way before writing. If we don't, we most likely won't retain everything we mean to write.

feature 4.2 Aristotle

As already noted, Aristotle's answer to what he saw as a problem with attention span was to advise speakers to rely on shortened patterns of reasoning (41, 42). Don't belabor what is obvious because most people become bored with being told what they already know. One example Aristotle gives concerns what was in the fourth century BCE common knowledge about the Olympics—knowledge we now no longer have, of course. Aristotle writes, "[to show] that Dorieus has won a contest with a crown it is enough to have said that he has won the Olympic games, and there is no need to add that the Olympic games have a crown as the prize; for everybody knows that" (42).

Obviously, it is not good practice to belabor the obvious. Get to the conclusion. This was part of Aristotle's view on rhetoric. And it suggests, incidentally, that quite probably Aristotle would not have enjoyed listening to the typical five paragraph theme, given all of its needless repetition.

There are certainly differences between writing and speaking in public. As Aristotle noted, in the case of a speech, we might be limited in how much new information we can expect an audience to remember. In ancient times, when most people did not read, speakers and poets would rely on rhyming patterns or repetition to help audience members to remember more easily what was said. And they would rely on commonplaces and shortened forms of reasoning. We see both of these practices often enough today in advertising language that is short, clipped, rhythmic, catchy, and based on "common sense."

feature 4.3

Argument and Joining the Conversation

We might compare writing to the public speech. The audience for a speech is always in front of us, concrete. The audience for writing, though not immediately vivid as an audience to a speech, is just as concrete. We need to use our imaginations to reflect on the readers we want to address.

In thinking about who our audience might be for our writing, a metaphor might clarify why invention is so valuable, the metaphor of a conversation. It is not original with me. In fact, it is valued by many artists and speakers who are attuned to the social aspects of speaking, writing, and literacy. In the following famous passage, Kenneth Burke compares the acts of thinking and writing to someone entering a room and trying to join in the conversation there:

Imagine that you enter a parlor. You come late. When you arrive, others have long preceded you, and they are engaged in a heated discussion, a discussion too heated for them to pause and tell you exactly what it is about. In fact, the discussion had already begun long before any of them got there, so that no one present is qualified to retrace for you all the steps that had gone before. You listen for a while, until you decide that you have caught the tenor of the argument; then you put in your oar. Someone answers; you answer him; another comes to your defense; another aligns himself against you, to either the embarrassment or gratification of your opponent, depending upon the quality of your ally's assistance. However, the discussion is interminable. The hour grows late, you must depart. And you do depart, with the discussion still vigorously in progress. (Burke 110–111)

Reflect on the situation Burke describes in this passage. It might be considered the universal conversation of humanity, a way of seeing the push and pull of some historical human struggle going on far longer than can be known. On another level, as well, one which honors the first and is connected to it, surely everyone has experienced walking into the middle of a compelling conversation but not quite knowing where it is going or where it has been. To get involved, we first may need to hear a few things before we "put in our oar," a phrase some have suggested is a pun on "or," as when we suggest, "Or it could be like this." The idea captured here applies to writing, thinking, and speaking at any level. As we struggle to find what we have to say, we listen to the trend of the current conversation. That probably involves reading up on what has been said recently about our topic. We listen and gauge what has been said and even how it has been said. Then we add our bit before we find that the hour is late and we must leave it.

Consider how well this metaphor captures how to think about writing as a social act. As we begin writing, that is, joining the conversation, first we listen to how the subject is being discussed when we enter. We learn first what we do and do not know, as well as, perhaps, what our fellow conversationalists do and do not know. We may need to fill in background for ourselves, ask questions, seek definitions.

Writing as Social

Thinking about writing in terms of the metaphor of joining a conversation underscores our connection to others, even in an act that seems solitary. Even after I enter a room alone and close the door, I still carry with me the voices of those who have influenced me in various ways. And most of what I will write in that private place will be heard by others and taken into their lives. So literacy is perhaps best thought of and practiced as a social art. Not only do we want to know what is being said. We want to add to what is being said. Through reflection and careful reading, we want to add new knowledge to the mix. If we choose to begin our writing without this reflection, we will most likely find ourselves simply restating platitudes or commonsense notions that tell our readers what they know already. Or we will expose ourselves as being uninformed and not worthy of being listened to—as irrelevant to the human conversation. The metaphor of "joining the conversation" might help us to reconsider our beliefs about writing and, perhaps, change our practice.

What Is Rhetoric? Differing Definitions

Perhaps the social commonplaces that writers and speakers use are most characteristic of the way Aristotle, at least, discusses rhetoric, though the first idea that may come to mind when we hear the word "rhetoric" is "fluff." Or perhaps we will think of empty, even fanciful terms divorced from reality. As such, rhetoric is the opposite of what we have come to associate with "plain speaking." In popular usage, the term may be more commonly viewed as a synonym for false, inflated language employed especially by used car dealers or politicians from the "other party," whose intent is to deceive. Especially when politicians say things that sound positive or pleasing, we suspect that they are only "engaging in rhetoric" and not telling the truth. Instead of using a more accurate term for this, such as "euphemism," "double speak," "inflated language," or simply "lying," we use the term "rhetoric." Rhetoric is a pretentious, negative attempt to use words to deceive.

But as suggested above, Aristotle's view of rhetoric is similar to philosophy. To discover what he is talking about, we might begin by unpacking his definition.

Finding "Available Means"

Aristotle called rhetoric "an ability, in each particular case, to see the available means of persuasion" (36). There is something of Burke's idea of entering the parlor in this Greek idea of coming together to argue in the *polis* or city center.

In this setting, different men would argue for and against an idea or proposal, and then the hearers would judge among these arguments to determine the best reasons for the best possible position to take. Just prior to giving his tentative definition of rhetoric, Aristotle says that its function "is not to persuade but to see the available means of persuasion in each case" (35). This suggests that rhetoric is designed for us to hear critically the various arguments on any topic. In doing this, we can determine the best position. Like philosophers listening to a dialectic between two or three possible positions, rhetoricians listen to two or three possible views on an issue of concern to everyone.

Aristotle begins with the idea that rhetoric is something that all people can be observed doing. Most do it out of habit or without thinking too much about how it is done; we argue back and forth, struggling for the upper hand in our disagreements. But there is the possibility that we can be taught to do it well, Aristotle suggests. So he saw rhetoric as a public art that, at its best, was not focused on using flowery language, but on forms of reason used in the making of arguments. These forms concern certain kinds of proof, which he calls "artistic" because they are made up or invented by the speaker. These form the area of study or habits, Aristotle suggests, or the practice that can lead to persuasiveness.

It should be added that the second part to Aristotle's definition points to an important part of this art: to see the "available means of persuasion" in particular, not universal, cases. It is to discover both what is already known to an audience and what might be possible as new knowledge. This makes invention relevant not only to what one particular audience knows already about an issue—what it believes and is willing to consider about it—but also to what new possibilities are available. The proofs the rhetor will construct—logical proofs, emotional proofs, and proofs of character or *ethos*—will be determined by their persuasiveness to an audience, rooted in what an audience understands to be true in a given case. "Finding the available means of persuasion" will be about how effectively a speaker can use this common understanding to persuade a particular group to new possibilities. As one commentator has suggested, the exciting, even exhilarating aspects of public speeches that are well done have this about them: they show both speaker and audience poised in a place of discovery between what has been known and what is possible (Sullivan 607).

To avoid a tendency to think that Aristotle's views on rhetoric are no different than ours, a few differences between our world and his should be kept in mind. First, the ancients did not look at language in terms of one form of it conveying truth and the other form conveying rhetoric or lies. Rhetoric could, at least according to Aristotle, be used in the interests of what he would have called "the truth." And, as one scholar has suggested, theatrical productions could be concerned with arguments (Rosenmeyer). Also, a difference between the world we now inhabit and the worlds of ancient Greece and Rome, where rhetoric first flourished, concerns the public nature of argument. To the ancients, speaking about issues of importance and writing about them were not private concerns.

This is an important emphasis to keep in mind: unlike our current ways of thinking about writing as a private activity, ancient thinkers considered rhetoric to be public. Even poetry in the ancient world was considered the public expression of collective values, images, and virtues. Aristotle's teaching about rhetoric is still relevant, especially teachings about the use of reason, the use of emotion, and the appeal of an ethical character. And they weren't thought of as mechanical formulas or exercises, either. As Aristotle observed, as he notes at the beginning of his book on rhetoric, the artistic proofs—*logos, pathos,* and *ethos*—were proofs readily observable to the average citizen involved in public discourse.

Artistic Proofs: Alive, Well, and Interrelated

The three artistic proofs, *logos, pathos,* and *ethos,* can be seen working together in most acts of persuasion. The more effective uses of *logos,* or the logical appeal, will be tempered with appeals to character.

The logical appeal is generally understood to consist of appeals to an audience's reason or to uses of inductive or deductive reasoning. Aristotle included in this the use of signs or indicators of certain conditions. For example, a recent school shooting could be given by a writer as a sign of trouble and exposure to violence among youth, though not as proof of anything—though some writers have seized on school shootings as proof that video games have become too violent. Long lines at the unemployment service could be given as a sign of a bad economy. As Augustine points out, there are cultural signs as well as natural ones. Writers may employ signs to draw attention to an issue.

But as noted earlier in this chapter, the logical appeal Aristotle spends most of his time on concerns the shortened form of deductive reasoning called the "enthymeme," a syllogism that has been shortened by leaving one of the premises or the conclusion unstated. The enthymeme is effective for two reasons. It allows the speaker or writer to draw on the premises that might be shared with an audience, a premise that might really be an assumption and not well established. Consider, for example the premise that "all only children grow up spoiled and don't know how to share with others." This might form the basis for an argument that a man or woman might make that they should have more than one child. The speaker may never make this statement directly, but it will be clear in statements such as this one: "We don't want our child to grow up alone and selfish. We should give him a brother or sister or two." The unstated major premise of the longer syllogism, stated above, is in full force in this argument as an assumption this couple holds about how children learn to share.

Again, this assumption might not have any real evidence to support it, but it is still powerful as ideology. The effective speaker will look at, or "see," assumptions like this one to understand the values and beliefs of an audience, and whether or not a need exists for more evidence to change or challenge such an assumption. Appeals to helping the poor can work this way. On one hand, we might find ourselves appealing to audiences who believe that the poor have brought their destitute conditions on themselves. In this particular case, it would appear that the best we can do is to let the poor fend for themselves and, as the saying goes, "pull themselves up by their own bootstraps." In contrast, there are those who are convinced that government programs are the best way to help the homeless, that we show our compassion as a nation by having compassionate government programs. As a writer, you may agree with one or the other of these views, or you may share neither. But if you are trying to persuade your readers to care for the poor, you will want to "see" both of these views, consider them as you create your reasons for what you believe should be done.

As Aristotle observed, in those debates that matter most to us, logic is not always an "available means." More often, we are persuaded also through the force of a good character, or at least the appeal of a character who means well. And just as often, people respond more strongly than they ought to when subjected to emotional appeals. However, because we can be just as repelled by appeals to *pathos* in pictures of starving children as we can be moved by them, appeals to *pathos* are best used carefully. Much depends upon other factors, especially if some organizations claiming to help the poor have been found not to. The appeal to *pathos* is perhaps best used when we sense greater appeals to logic being used.

In a similar way, the character of a speaker can work against him or her. So we might consider Hillary Clinton's appeal to *ethos* during the historic 2008 Democratic presidential primary season, in which she asserted that she was the candidate with experience. As a former First Lady, then senator, and presidential candidate, Clinton, in speaking to voters in the Iowa primary for the 2008 Democratic presidential race, was widely known as an intelligent, even brilliant woman. To some, this *ethos* was part of her appeal, and to some it was negative. As well, there was her marriage to a former president who was both popular and controversial. In her campaign, she tried to turn to good persuasive effect her eight years as First Lady and her major role in her husband's failed initiative to provide a form of universal health care in the early 1990s. This was also an argument she was making against a particular opponent, whose new and hopeful speeches sounded much like her husband's in his first presidential campaign, but who could also be cast as untested and inexperienced. Clinton's creation in her speeches of her experienced *ethos* did not work, however, as Iowa voters were clearly more motivated by a desire for change than for experience, which they took to mean more of the same old thing. When they voted for both Barack Obama and John Edwards ahead of Clinton, she had to make changes to her message to better fit what could be the available means of persuasion in the New Hampshire primary. There, her mantra kept the sound of experience, but it also placed emphasis on it in a more nuanced way: "You campaign in poetry," she said. "You govern in prose."

Clinton's changing appeals might be seen as examples of rhetoric at its worst, as political sloganeering and changing words to meet expectations. Yet what might also be seen here is an adjustment Clinton felt she had to make in her appeal to *ethos*, especially to making her theme of experience more into an "available means of persuasion."

It should be stressed regarding the appeal to character, or *ethos,* that its opposite, that is, the attack against the character of opponents, so common in recent presidential elections, is not some altered form of *ethos*. Rather, making attacks against an opponent's character is considered a logical fallacy, called *ad hominem,* which is Latin for "to the man." Though recent candidates have gotten away with using this fallacy and even benefited from it, it is not considered ethical. Indeed, the possibility always exists that what have come to be called "negative attack ads" will reflect badly on the character of the one making them. Attacking one's opponents does not improve one's *ethos*. It can undermine it.

Types of Argument

Aristotle's first concern in his presentation on rhetoric has to do with the speaker's preparation, with what she will have to say that will be compelling and convincing to a particular, given audience. This is the main concern of invention, of finding arguments or, as stated previously, of "seeing what are the available means of persuasion in each case." It should also be understood that Aristotle was writing mainly about oral presentations, not written ones. His advice has to do with preparing a case for public speaking, as a lawyer would in a court case, though Aristotle saw three main occasions for public speaking—*forensic, epidiectic*, and *deliberative*. We might begin by thinking of them in this way: forensic speeches involved court cases concerned with matters of guilt or innocence; epidiectic speeches concerned ceremonial occasions of praise or blame, occasions where certain values might be celebrated or reaffirmed; deliberative speeches might have concerned matters of public or foreign policy or governance.

Each of these three forms of persuasion could be further subdivided. It is also true that we might find occasions where two or more might be blended, as when a community leader calls on her community to fight crime and also extols the virtue of courage. But clearly, each form calls for preparation, especially given the ceremonial or public call for decorum in each, where the speaker's *ethos* might be strengthened or undermined by the very performance of the speech—or, for that matter, the writing.

Today, such ceremony might seem artificial, unless we are witnessing the funeral of a president, a memorial after a tragic event like one of the space shuttle disasters, or the opening of the Olympic games. But where we observe ceremonial pomp and circumstance happening when it seems unearned, it becomes grounds for parody or satire. In fact, the success of much public speaking today depends on the speaker's ability to connect with democratic audiences, who are quick to detect pretentiousness and and judge those moments as occasions for mockery. Even so, this does not mean that the speaker does not need to prepare before speaking or writing. It simply means that today, the occasions for speaking are not always clearly mapped out and defined in terms of purpose. Still, what an audience expects is still important, and rules of decorum are still in effect.

Another issue is that teachings about invention today might apply to written rather than spoken discourse. Though this leads to a need for observing written conventions (paragraphing, sentence length, documentation, mechanical concerns, grammar, and spelling), most of the initial concerns for public speaking and audience still apply. Though the audience for writing may seem vague or unclear or (maybe) one's teacher, the public metaphor of an audience, of people who belong to communities and who have values and needs, is a valuable one to keep in mind. In fact, many published writers (note the shared root in the words "published" and "public," the Latin word *publein*) talk of imagining certain people or audiences as they are writing. Indeed, though it might seem to require some imagination, the act of writing is hardly a solitary activity. When we sit down to write, we often carry with us the voices of our family, friends, classmates, and former teachers. Though it is perhaps good advice to ignore our audience at first as we begin to write, there does come a time when we also will need to consider who our audience will be.

The constraints we may already feel as writers when given an assignment that includes a long list of teacher requirements might already seem daunting. Yet skipping over the planning involved in invention only makes the act of writing seem even more impossible. Instead, we might consider how invention might help us as we begin writing. In this chapter, before moving on to greater detail in concerns with particular assignments or purposes, I would like to suggest a map that we might follow in order to better refine how we perform as writers. After all, writing is a performance, just as public speaking is, even if in writing the performance may seem silent and internalized and, in the final product, one that our readers might not see or hear for weeks, months, or even years after we have finalized it.

It is still a performance.

Starting Invention

In one sense, the Internet can seem to be an amazing tool, with a million pathways to a million parlor rooms buzzing with all the conversations and information you could possibly want, all available at a moment's click. But on another level, the Internet can be seen as staying on the surface of things.

The Internet also seems democratic for the way that it uncritically allows any opinion to take root. Some will assume that this means that all opinions are valid and equal. But all opinions are not equal. In fact, it is the point of rhetoric to test opinions and discover which are most probable. Given rhetoric, all opinions must hold up under questioning, analysis, and evidence to the contrary. In a very real sense, rhetoric is concerned with arguing over what we can sometimes only know in part. But it is meant to provide us with a method for examining what we believe. In addition to having our own opinions and beliefs, it is important that we know why we believe something; it is valuable if we can offer support for our opinions.

In his work on rhetoric, Aristotle held that it concerned what mattered most to us but could only be known in part. Most people, when arguing from common sense, do not necessarily state the basis of their thinking; much of this remains below the surface. He called these parts, both hidden assumptions or premises serving the unstated part of a larger chain of reasoning, and the reasoning itself, an enthymeme. For example, the statement "Of course Socrates is a mortal; after all, he's a man," has as its unstated premise the universally "acknowledged truth that all men (and women) are mortal." A more interesting example of the use of the enthymeme might be the one a seven-year-old used when she confronted her parents about the truth of the existence of Santa Claus. "Saint Nicholas died," she said. "And he didn't come back from the dead. So who is putting all those presents under our tree?" Implicit, unstated in her enthymeme was a version of the Socrates syllogism, to wit, that "all men are mortal" and therefore die and can't be around anymore to put presents under trees. Even her mother's assurances that "Santa has helpers" were met with skepticism. The girl turned and announced that she would not tell her younger sister about it. Clearly, the force of the seven-year-old's enthymeme was greater than any "fictions" her parents created about helpers.

Much of the reasoning people do about the important issues they face, over concerns with diversity, policies of war, welfare, or taxation, follow the same pattern used by this seven-year-old. In Aristotle's terms, it is the working habit of the speaker or writer on issues to examine the unstated support underlying such conclusions, opinions, or assumptions. This is a form of thinking critically on issues for which absolute, unshakable information, facts, or knowledge, is not forthcoming. In these cases, what people put forward as fact or certainty are beliefs or the result of certain experiences. The speaker or writer uses invention to reflect on and think about those beliefs, often with the hope of finding in those hidden assumptions some ground of agreement or shared knowledge. So the pro-choice advocate might begin a debate by showing that she values life; conversely, the pro-life advocate would do well to try to show that the health, safety, and welfare of the mother is a part of her pro-life perspective. Granted, in neither case, where the speaker faces a deeply committed belief system, are they likely to be persuasive. More will be required.

This points to the limitation of Aristotle's reason-centered view of rhetoric. For persuasion to happen in these cases, what is needed is some form of transformation, for the underlying, often hidden premises to be challenged and altered. But Aristotle was correct that beginning with the adversary's values might at least win a respectful hearing from our audience who will judge our position.

Clearly, it is important for the writer to question common sense, and to be reflective before writing. It is for this reason that most writing teachers advocate some form of invention that brings us not only to do research but also to think about the common opinions that are associated with the topic of concern. Of course, whether this first stage involves reflecting on hidden assumptions to generate new arguments or doing research through reading books and articles will depend on the nature of the particular case and how much we know about it. You may think that you can launch into your argument about why it's fine to download music from the Internet without paying for it, but do you really understand copyright laws or the arguments of the artists? You will best prepare yourself by listening to the artists before you formulate what you will say. You may need to reflect on your reading, weighing arguments before you decide to write.

The Structure Most Arguments Take, and Why

Argument is an important way of proving that an opinion you hold is persuasive. Typically, we argue over policy, over interpretation (Whitman's poem is about democratic values, or the Bible teaches that community is important to personal growth), over a position (generally, the right to have an abortion on demand should be respected and upheld), and over how to solve a problem (the solution to plagiarism is the new honors system being instituted at our school).

Generally, argument will be structured differently depending on the type of being made, on what you are arguing, and on your understanding of your audience's values and beliefs about the points being argued. Like the five-paragraph theme, argument has a beginning, middle, and end. This is what must happen in those three parts:

The Beginning

This captures the reader's interest and shows the scope or main point to be argued. And the thesis, or narrowed focus, is or can be given here, if you sense that the audience is ready to hear it. (Of course, if you are a pro-life advocate in front of a pro-choice crowd, you will probably want to hold this until your conclusion, as you first will want to build rapport with your audience, show how you understand their values, and give good reasons for our own position first.)

Middle

This has at least three parts. The first is the **anticipation of opposing views**, those main, important arguments against what you are advocating. Consider these views briefly, respectfully, without calling names or implying evil. Then **refute these views**, showing why they are wrong, irrelevant, or unconvincing because of evidence to the contrary. At this point you can also **concede to certain points in the opposition** as reasonable. Some concession shows you are reasonable and open to dialogue. Following this section, which can take up much of your essay or speech, build your own case for why your thesis is reasonable or true or the best course of action in solving the problem.

Building a case can also make up the bulk of your conclusion, which need not be signaled by "in conclusion, I have argued these four points." Other ways to conclude might include a quote, a return to the scenario given in your introduction (also known as framing), or speculating on two futures, the one where nothing is done and the one where your plan is adopted.

A Sample Argument

The following argument is fairly typical. It begins with a story in an attempt to draw the reader into the central issue. It addresses opposing views early in the paper, and only after doing this does it offer a thesis of what should be done at the end. In this thesis, the writer offers a change in public policy that many should find controversial. Read the argument and then conduct Burke's parlor. What do you find agreeable and, perhaps, disagreeable about it? Discuss this attempt to change public policy about movie attendance.

feature 4.4   An Argument on Violence and Media

The scene has stayed with me. Sonny Corleone, angry that his sister has again been abused by her husband, leaves the fortified compound of the Corleone family without bodyguards and drives to Long Island to pay his brother-in-law back for the beating. On the way, he stops to pay a toll, when suddenly the car in front of him stalls and men in dark coats with machine guns get out of the backseat. Others appear in the tollboth, and all start firing. The scene trumps anything reality offers because the camera focuses what the viewer sees—Sonny trying to escape out the passenger's side of his car while the bullets pierce the car, puncture his body and the car seats, and explode his flesh in every space he tries to duck into, until he falls out onto the tollway, where one of his enemies walks up to him, riddles his body with machine gun fire, making it leap like a snake, and then kicks Sonny's mutilated body.

I saw this scene from *The Godfather* after I turned sixteen. I had just gotten my driver's license and had driven some friends to see it—our first R-rated movie. What I also remember, however, is that it was not a movie we emerged from saying "wow" or "cool" or any of the other squeals of delight that adolescent boys make. None of us wanted to join a mob or start a gang or even start toting a gun. This was 1972, summer, and what I remember is our subdued, drained affect as we drove back to our suburb. We didn't talk much, but the images were playing over and over in my mind. And as I sought to come to terms with what I'd seen, I wondered what made me react as I did. Rather than descending into a maelstrom of violence and crime, I had a firmer conviction than before that violence was wrong, that to murder another was to somehow murder yourself, though I didn't say so at the time. Seeing the movie left me with a sadness that was deadening and persisted long after the movie's run ended at local theaters.

Today, as I think about this, I am convinced that at the time, my movie viewing (and music consumption and TV viewing) was a secondary influence. My primary influence was my family and, through them, Catholicism. My parents talked about certain values and had a personal ethic that satisfied me as having integrity.

So I could be saddened by violence mainly because my family was a cover for me. It seems a sound principle that the main protection for youth is to be found in the family. The troubling aspect of this, however, is that when I start to generalize to others today, this has sometimes been taken away, through divorce, through the death of a parent, or through parental incompetence. So when people argue that the answer to keeping kids from violence is the responsibility of the parents, they are both correct and mistaken at the same time. Something *feature 4.4 (cont.)*

more needs to be considered if we are to help today's youth confront what some politicians have called a "culture of violence."

In current discussions about violence and entertainment, some people will argue that American media perpetuate violence, especially the idea that violence is a way to solve all of our problems. This is Barbara Kingsolver's argument as she laments the tragic killings at Columbine High School. "Children model the behavior of adults," she writes, "on whatever scale is available to them. Ours are growing up in a nation whose most important, influential men—from presidents to the coolest film characters—solve problems by killing people" (416). Kingsolver asserts that it is probable that some youths "desperate for admiration and influence" will resort to violence (416).

Kingsolver's argument might, of course, seem right. And she avoids overgeneralizing—she doesn't say that all youths will resort to acts of violence. But there's something wrong in her assertion that what is being seen in the "coolest film characters" is the same thing that is happening in the world, and that two youths shot up their high school in Colorado because they saw everyone around them solving their problems that way. For Kingsolver, this is to oversimplify a complex issue and avoid some deeper issues that those youths must have faced with alienation, despair, and real-world sadness—real problems that ultimately make her call to establish "zero tolerance" for violence across our culture, a kind of cop-out (417). Kingsolver seems to want us to be against violence in principle without recognizing how to confront it when we see it in our culture. To "take a stand against violence in principle" may be all well and good, but it is finally to avoid real legislation that might make a difference in practical terms.

In reflecting on violence in our culture today, I've sometimes wondered what made my childhood different from those of the children I see around me today. Many adults I know are quick to say that children today face things we never had to face. But this may only be because of the parenting that passes for normal today. Certainly, we allow more graphic violence during family viewing hour on TV, which observers have noticed is being invaded more and more with adult situations. And every time I attend a movie that I will not allow my kids to see, I still find myself sitting near children whose parents have let them see it, sometimes very small children. Some of those children I see getting very frightened by certain images and scenes. Perhaps they are being desensitized, deadened, as I was that one summer.

feature 4.4 (cont.)

I would still argue that these forms of violent entertainment need not be censored, banned, as Kingsolver would apparently want to see happen. But I do wonder: if children are no longer covered, if the primary influence of the family has been taken away from them or become corrupt or lacking in integrity, what are they left with? Friends as dumb and inexperienced as they are? TV, movies, and music, the influence of which would otherwise be minor?

I'm inclined to argue that movie and television violence does not have to lead to children acting out that violence in their own lives, and that more often than not, it doesn't lead to anything but unearned cynicism and arrogant posturing, the sort of thing that might eventually result in chronic, real despair—perhaps especially for kids for whom movies, TV, and music have replaced the saner, more intelligent, interactive voices of their elders.

I believe the problem for most youth today is that the elders are silenced or ridiculed. This is all the more reason for vigilance at the box office. What I would advocate is some stringent change in a few places where it matters most. First, levy heavy fines against networks that taint the family viewing time, the period from about 6:00 to 9:00 p.m., with adult material—even commercials for adult material. The most vigilant parent is defenseless against these onslaughts. But second, start treating movie theaters the way we treat bars and taverns. Levy hefty fines when children are caught getting into movies that the ratings system has warned they shouldn't. Perhaps both theaters and parents should be made to pay.

Children should not be allowed into R or even PG-13 movies. If directors refuse to make PG movies, they've automatically lost part of their audience. Children should not be given a steady diet of despair, alienation, posturing, and bloodshed. If the parents are gone, these children become wards of the state in more ways than one. And that means that we can recoup some tax money in the interests of some real prevention.

Works Cited

Kingsolver, Barbara. "Life Is Precious, or It's Not." *Language Awareness: Readings for College Writers.* Ed. Paul Eschholz, Alfred Rosa, and Virginia Clark. 9th ed. Boston: St. Martin's, 2005: 415–417.

Discussion Questions

1. Why does this writer begin the essay with a story? What is the nature of this story, and why might it be effective? Does it set up the argument that follows?
2. What does this writer mean in the third paragraph by "primary" and "secondary influences"? And how do these terms work in his argument?
3. Does the writer consider real opposition views here? List others that might need to be considered if the writer is going to be persuasive to the audience.
4. What objections might be raised to the writer's proposal here to change public policy about movie ratings and attendance?

Practice with Rhetoric—Rehearsing for Paper One

Over the next week, divide the members of your class in half and prepare to stage three debates, one deliberative, one epideictic, and one forensic. Each side of the classroom must take the opposing view of the other on the following issues (1) Deliberative: whether a policy that concerns them as students in college, in the dorms, in student life, is helpful or hurtful and should be changed

feature 4.5

© 2009 by easyshoot. Used under license of Shutterstock, Inc.

in some way. They also need to demonstrate that this policy is really harmful or helpful, even worth debating about. *Example*: whether to change some policy with English writing placement at the university. (2) Whether plagiarism is a violation we should be vigilant to police against as students. (3) Whether our high school teachers were guilty of teaching us mechanical writing skills. For each one, students must formulate a clear argumentative thesis or statement, pro or con. Students must present as clearly as possible all of their arguments in as much detail as possible for their side. They must be aware of inventing artistic arguments of *logos, ethos,* and *pathos.* They must also show awareness of possible opposing views.

After an initial presentation, each side will be allowed to address the opposition's objections. Then a panel of judges will state which side gave the best reasons for their position. Finally, all in class will be allowed to state what their final view on each argument is after having heard all sides.

For Further Discussion

feature 4.6　Writing Prompt Reflection

Considering the ideas in Writing Prompt 4, write an argument about it. Is television to blame for shortened attention spans and bad writing? Construct your own response.

Ethos Considered

1. As a class, evaluate the ethos of the following public figures. Account for what makes up their positive or negative impression for you and your group.

    Barack Obama
    Hillary Clinton
    Angelina Jolie
    Bono
    Eminem
    Your last English teacher

2. Why might spelling and grammar knowledge be important to a writer's *ethos*? Explain, arguing for or against.

3. Talking back to the text: Choose any one of the sections in this chapter and show why you disagree with it or why it is true. Be prepared to defend your position.

Works Cited

Aristotle. *On Rhetoric: A Theory of Civic Discourse*. Trans. George A. Kennedy. New York: Oxford UP, 1991.

Augustine. *On Christian Doctrine*. Trans. J. F. Shaw. Chicago: Encyclopedia Britannica, 1952.

Burke, Kenneth. "The Philosophy of Literary Form." *The Philosophy of Literary Form: Studies in Symbolic Action*. Berkley: U. of California P., 1973: 1–137.

Crowley, Sharon, and Debra Hawhee. *Ancient Rhetorics for Contemporary Students*. 4th ed. New York: Pearson/Longman, 2009.

Kellog, Ronald. "Acquiring Advanced Writing Skills: A View from Cognitive Science." Conference on College Composition and Communication, 11–14 Mar 2009, San Francisco, CA.

Rosenmeyer, Thomas G. "Gorgias, Aeschylus, and *Apate*." *American Journal of Philology* 76.3 (1955): 225–260.

Sullivan, Dale. "Rhetorical Invention and Lutheran Doctrine?" *Rhetoric & Public Affairs* 7.4 (Winter 2004): 603–614.

Grammar Interlude 4: Modifiers

MODIFIERS

Other major parts of speech...

What you most need to know as a writer about modifiers has to do with simple addition and subtraction. When you think you are adding to your description—using an adjective, for example, to spice up a noun—you may actually be doing the opposite and subtracting from your noun's semantic power. Use them sparingly and surprisingly. Listen to the words playing in your thoughts.

1. **ADJECTIVES** add to nouns (but often subtract from their power, especially when they are clichés).

    Red bus
    Famous writer
    Celebrated rock band

    EX. 1. Go back to EX. 1. In Chapter 1 and add adjectives to your five sentences.

2. **ADVERBS**, words usually ending in -ly, add to verbs (but often subtract from their power, when they are clichés).

    EX. 2. Sarah yelled loudly. (Is this adverb really needed? Can't just "yelled" carry the action? Has anyone ever yelled quietly?) Please try to think about the phrases tumbling out of your mind.

3. **PREPOSITIONAL PHRASES**

    Prepositions are small words of direction. Many handbooks list dozens of them. Examples include: at, on, over, of, in, above, under, until. With nouns, prepositions form prepositional phrases.

    At the show
    On the stove
    Over the water
    Of the five going
    In the park

    These phrases can modify other words.

    Ex. 3. Find the prepositional phrases in the following and explain which word or words they modify.

1. The ducks in the park can be seen sleeping on the lawn every morning.
2. At the time, Phil was working for NASA in the administration.
3. The house on the corner with the white fence and a fountain on the lawn has three bedrooms and two baths.

Chapter *Five*

Writing the Evaluation and Opinion Essay

Chapter Overview

Chapter 5 continues a focus begun in Chapter 4 on commonplaces, moving to why opinions are important to writing. The chapter begins with a focus on why opinions are as important as facts to a writer and how we should reflect honestly on our opinions. This leads to a discussion of two kinds of writing that deal with opinions—evaluations and opinion essays.

Consider how we use opinions.

To state their case in an argument, people often begin with the words, "in my opinion," but then they rarely stop to provide evidence.

Opinions are cheap, certainly. As the saying goes, everyone has one. Even so, what is not commonly understood about them deserves attention.

An Opinion about Opinions

Consider the following example.

"In my opinion, President Nixon was very shrewd to abolish the military draft."

Again, the opening phrase here can be heard all the time. But is it necessary for the speaker to tell the reader that she is offering an opinion? If one wrote simply, "Nixon was shrewd to abolish the military draft," is it suddenly, magically no longer an opinion? Because there can apparently be more than one view on Nixon's motives when he did away with the draft in the early 1970s, it is pretty clear that this constitutes a difference of opinion, one that requires evidence.

But it may be that having to provide evidence is what many writers hope to avoid. Some believe that they don't have to give evidence for their opinions. Stating "this is just my opinion" seems, on the one hand, the equivalent of a footnote. On the other, it seems to suggest a view of knowledge that is deeply personal, based in experience, and drawn from parents, friends, and from living. Who can challenge that?

Most academics do.

Writing Is Different from Speaking

Part of what is going on may have to do with confusion over the differences between speaking and writing. The conflicting advice many people often get about writing is interesting. "Just write naturally, the way you talk" and "Don't write the way you talk" constitute at least one important contradiction many people hear as advice. Certainly, the best stylists know how to approximate speech while remaining true to Standard Written English. They create a highly readable and engaging "conversational" style. But this takes a great deal of work and study. No writer just writes exactly as she speaks. A transcribed conversation is a messy, incongruous puzzle, even to the people who conducted it. They look back at it and wonder what they meant.

In matters of opinion, speech conventions and writing conventions differ widely. When talking, I can say, "but in my opinion," and my friend, unless she is a university colleague and we are together serving on a committee, will not expect evidence to follow. But in writing, I will need to give good reasons for my opinion.

Genre Confusion

Many people believe that what works in conversation—"but that's just my opinion"—will work in writing. Some posting on social networking sites also appear to believe that posting slogans and clichés over and over again will eventually result in their readers having a sudden revelation of the truth of their views. But this is a very low view they hold of their readers—to think of them as only needing to be shouted at. More likely, their readers are waiting for evidence.

It is true that in casual speech, we may not want a friend to engage in a long "dissertation" with us or a harangue. "In my humble opinion" seems, in polite conversation, appropriate. But in writing, "in my opinion" is usually a wordy flag to an unsupported assertion. As a reader, I might be charmed by a writer's opinion, especially if it is a daring one. But I also expect to be charmed by the writer's reasons for his or her opinion.

But this is not the same as saying that an opinion has no value in writing, or that it is less important than facts.

Facts seem self-evident and objective. When pressed in an argument, many people will claim that they are only stating the facts. This is the same thing as saying that there is no argument, that the facts "speak for themselves" and establish what is true.

Only when we really start to look at them do facts seem hard to pin down. When pressed for a definition, many people will say that a fact is the opposite of an opinion. As noted in Writing Prompt 5, this is the way that news anchors on television will often feature stories, with titles like: "A Cover-up on Wall Street: Fact or Myth?" But if we say that fact is the opposite of myth, what are we saying? What is a fact? Usually, by "fact," we mean those settled aspects of our experiences that no reasonable mind will dispute. In school, facts are those always-correct answers on any test.

Yet, consider. Some facts can change—or perhaps they are not facts. It was settled "fact" during the time of Sir Isaac Newton that traveling faster than thirty miles per hour would result in suffocation. That Newton is reported to have believed that humans would one day travel in horseless carriages at speeds reaching sixty miles per hour opened him to ridicule by his contemporary, Voltaire. This might sound like the ignorance of an early, prescientific culture, but consider that presently, the fantasies of *Star Trek* and *Star Wars* not withstanding, our best theories in physics currently lead us to the conclusion that it is impossible to travel the speed of light. We have theories of relativity to account for changes in time and energy as we approach light speed. As more evidence comes in, our "facts" can and probably will change.

It is currently a widely held belief that the Inuit peoples of Alaska have many more words for snow than English speakers of the continental United States. I have heard this asserted as a fact even among scholarly and academic people, and yet it simply isn't true. The Inuit peoples have no more words for snow than the average Floridian. This "fact" was first announced at an academic gathering of linguists, where it was stated and then repeated among colleagues with none of them caring to check up on it. That the Inuit peoples had hundreds of words to account for the different kinds of snow in their environment seemed right. It fit with certain cultural theories academics were forming about how language and environment interact, but it wasn't based on research.

I've heard this idea circulated often in polite, and even academic, conversations as a "fact," that is, as settled and not open to argument, even a "fact" used to settle other arguments. How many more "facts" are there like this? The idea has gained great traction that people who have grown up as the only child, without siblings, are more selfish and hard to get along with than children who grow up having to share their parents and their toys with siblings. No one ever asks for evidence to support this notion. It seems intuitively correct that a child

feature 5.1   Writing Prompt 5

The Not So Simple Matter of Facts and Opinions

Televised newscasts will sometimes air features on an aspect of the daily news, allowing journalists to cover a story in greater depth than can be accomplished in a headline story. So, for example,a feature will be announced before a commercial break as "Liberal College Profs Specializing in Indoctrination: Fact or Fiction?" This announcement for an investigative story promises to present the subject as an either/or dilemma—reducing it for viewers to a simple matter of a single choice, as fact or fiction. (Sometimes the word "myth" is used as a synonym for "fiction." But the desired meaning is the same. Facts are preferred. Fiction is equated with myth or a story that is factually untrue.).

Notice the usage of these terms, which seem to be presented as objective, or value-neutral. The news, or so the implication runs, is simply doing its job in presenting the facts. But are these categories, especially when placed in opposition, really value neutral? Are news casters "just stating the facts"?

The first problem here is that either/or dilemma. Two choices are available. Fact is posed in contrast to fiction. Furthermore, as the issue in question is being framed as either a matter of fact, and therefore to be accepted as true, or fiction, that is, something fabricated, something close to a lie or a deception, the two categories are ranked. Over and against the facts as the journalist will give them and stand behind them, there is the question of fictions or myths, which can only be read at best as weak, wishful thinking, and at worst as deception. This framework is certainly not value neutral but instead suggests that facts are most important and to be contrasted, not with alternate accounts or other possibilities, but with fictions or, worse, made up deceptions. In fact, it may not be pressing matters too far to suggest that current ways of thinking may be such that facts are preferred to truth, with a capital or a small *t*.

Certainly, the either/or dilemma serves an ideological purpose for the journalist in ranking what she or he considers "real" knowledge. This presentation, used for many feature stories on news programs, is almost more significant than the subject being examined through this frame.

In this example, either all professors are liberal activists who try to indoctrinate their students, or the very idea that there are liberal, activist professors who flunk students who don't agree with them is all made up—the fictions of activist, right-wing extremists. Of course, might it not also be reasonable to find some sort of middle ground here, to say that there might be some liberal and some right-wing professors? And that some students might have trouble with their *feature 5.1*   Writing Prompt 5 (continued)

professors, of either left or right, who make agreeing with their convictions part of passing the course?

The related problem with this way of framing knowledge is that it uncritically propagates assumptions about the importance of a pseudo-scientific view of facts. However, with most issues, the facts can be hard to ascertain, and with some issues, the facts can be read in more than one way. Furthermore, with many issues that matter to people, opinions must be argued and debated. Though with science we claim to value facts, opinion is often what we have to work with, and more often than not, facts are read through arguments about differing opinions. Scientitsts submit all theories to a scientific method before arriving at conclusions, and even these conclusions, which some refer to as facts, might be debated again later.

But to say that we have either facts or opinions (that is, myths or fictions) is an oversimplified way of viewing the way that people think. And to assert that facts are more important than opinions is to assert an idea that is relatively new in Western culture.

who never has to share her parents' affection or her toys with siblings will grow up believing that she is the only person in the universe. In fact, studies of only children have largely refuted the idea that an only child is harder to get along with. In fact, an only child is often more accommodating, or just as accommodating and willing to share as an oldest child. But when I share these study results with others when conversing about this issue—for many parents, in fact, the reason for having more children after the first one is to make sure that their first one isn't selfish—they generally are skeptical of the study, so entrenched are their cultural views, based largely on a common sense view of things.

Sexist and racist notions have often been asserted as fact. In many movies and television shows, even as late as the 1970s, it was common to assert as a "fact" that men were more reasonable than women, who were depicted as too governed by emotional attachments. Western literature is full of these stereotypes, as well as racist notions that people of various ethnicities or races will behave in certain predetermined ways due to ethnic or racial profiling. These also were held as fact, and yet it is easy now to recognize that they were based on prejudice and hatred.

While the examples given here indicate that "fact" is sometimes more culturally based and open to question than we like to believe, certainly facts exist. The height of Mount Everest, for example, or the fact that President William Clinton signed NAFTA into law during his first term as president, or the distance of the nearest stars to Earth, the greatest depths of the Pacific Ocean, and what pressures those depths can exact—these are called facts, though even these (except, perhaps, for President Clinton's signing of NAFTA) are revised in the newest encyclopedias when better methods of measurement are devised. And even concerning NAFTA, it might be questioned whether Clinton would have signed it into law under different circumstances.

Consider how the facts play out in the complicated, divisive abortion debate in recent U.S. politics, particularly the disputed "fact" of when life begins. Positions various voters take on the abortion debate often seem elaborated around the "scientific" idea that life actually does not begin at conception, though this fact seems caught up in the ideological perspective of the individual. The trouble with the "facts" in this case, of course, is that medical and biological specialists disagree over when life begins. Little is settled by an appeal to "the facts."

It also appears that facts are not always interesting or relevant. It may be true that Mount Everest is so many feet high, but unless we are planning to scale it in the next year, a geologist doing related research, or a gambler placing a bet on a dog team going up it for some reason, the height of Mount Everest is not a fact with much relevance to anything that matters to us. This is true of many of the facts we believe inform our world.

The same is not true of opinions, which are open to discussion and debate. In fact, in a democratic society, debates must occur over opinions and what is probable knowledge. This, Aristotle noted, is why we have rhetoric. It is not that we want to always win these debates and, therefore, emerge as the victor, the one who is right. Rather, debating over opinions is one way of arriving at those opinions that are closer to the way things stand than others. We are engaging in these debates to arrive at the most reasonable position possible right now. The desire to be right, certainly, is a strong motive behind many arguments. In an intense debate, we may insist that we are only stating "the facts," when in reality we are really giving our most entrenched opinions. Perhaps it is more reasonable to understand that in many of the most important issues we face, in issues that often concern public policies, as Aristotle has observed, we only know things with a degree of probability. And yet, we need to act, we need to make decisions.

A number of commentators on Aristotle's rhetoric and on classical rhetoric in general have noted that, as Sharon Crowley and Debra Hawhee write, the ancients held opinion and commonplaces in higher esteem than we seem to today in a scientific culture (9). Traditionally, the three proofs in classical rhetoric, as outlined by Aristotle, did not consist only of facts, nor even only of reason. And they would not have relied solely on a good quote or maxim. The three, *logos,* or the appeal to reason, *ethos,* the appeal of a good and beneficent character, and *pathos,* the appeal to relevant and appropriate emotions, Aristotle outlined these on the idea that we are not merely persuaded by reason. Certainly, a careful examination can reveal that persuasion is not only based on reason, and that we hold some of our most important views on the basis of commitments we have become convinced are good.

Aristotle very clearly preferred the artistic proof of *logos,* or reason, over the others, though he was quick also to recognize that in the event that there is no compelling evidence at hand, *ethos* remains more persuasive than reason.

The ancients seemed to grasp the communal, shared aspects of beliefs and values and how these informed persuasion about cases in which only probable knowledge was available. They valued the commonplace, the probable, the opinion for reasons we may no longer understand. As Crowley and Hawhee suggest, the ancients would have considered an opinion to be not something personally held, but rather something drawn from and understood as having its origins in community and communal wisdom. Although we may often hear that it is not correct to argue over politics or religion in polite society, the idea probably being that such arguments concern deeply held personal opinions, the ancients would have disagreed. To them, issues of politics and religion would have been seen not as personal choices but as public, civic concerns. They would have valued the coming together of different mindsets to argue over opinion, because this would have been a way of getting at what were the better opinions, that is, those that accounted for the whole picture.

Where we think that opinions are personal and not open to contradiction, the ancients saw ideas held in community. The commonplace represented a kind of cultural and communal value or probability, and opening them up to consideration was one way of looking at the different values in a community, the different values held by an audience, and therefore the different ways to persuade an audience to a particular course of action. The Greek term for opinion, *doxa,* was used by Aristotle in his treatise on rhetoric to denote an area of opinion and community experience that could constitute an "available means of persuasion." Looking at the commonplace views held by others on a topic of important debate could lead to valuable ways to present evidence and persuade others that one's view was worth hearing and considering.

Opinions Matter I: Evaluations and Reviews

Some opinions really don't concern us much. One person loves blue cheese dressing, while another prefers ranch. Some think that *Gone With the Wind* was the greatest movie ever made; others think it a crashing bore. Obviously, in both cases, deeply personal tastes are at work; arguing about our favorite dressing might help others to understand our tastes better, certainly, and that is worth a discussion. The same is true of talking about the merits of *Gone With the Wind*. But for the most part, arguing about both dressing and our favorite movie, if only to bring someone over to our side of things, will be difficult—unless those we wish to persuade are open to our arguments.

An argument about our favorite actor, dressing, or type of car will involve our specifying how we determine what our favorite is. What criteria must be met for something to be our favorite? These will help those we are persuading to think about their own criteria. When we ask about criteria, we can debate about favorites, because most people will hold different—indeed, sometimes radically different—sets of criteria. These debates can sometimes change our minds, even sometimes deepen our thinking as we clarify new criteria. Of course, for the individual who can't get past the cheese mold in blue cheese dressing, no amount of words will be persuasive.

Consider, for example, the claim that Jack Nicholson is a great actor. The assertion could be based on personal taste. If one likes his kind of acting and the movies he acts in, then sure, he's great. On the other hand, saying that Nicholson is a great actor is quite a different thing from saying Nicholson is "my favorite actor," as blue cheese is "my favorite dressing." If we put it that way, as "a great actor," we move to a realm of more publicly shared criteria. While I might be left alone to cherish my favorite actors, my saying that someone is a great actor could be argued. What would the argument be based on? These same questions would arise in our discussion about whether or not the three most recent Star Wars movies were better than the earlier movies starring Harrison Ford, Mark Hamil, and Carrie Fisher, or the argument that the new John Grisham novel is a good novel.

The debate—our arguments—in each of these cases, will be centered on criteria. First it will center around what we decide are the main criteria, or list of requirements, for how we determine what great acting is, or what a great movie or a great novel is. The criteria will center around what is important to our values. Some people, most members of the Academy Awards nominating committee, would never accept a movie in the fantasy or science fiction genre as a nominee for Best Picture. Conservative critics specializing in advocating family viewing and what is appropriate for children spend a great deal of time reflecting on appropriateness of the content, though they may be among the first to notice character development and the depiction of meaningful relationships. Many moviegoers, at the same time, miss the "good old" days when the Best Picture category could still include popular movies and not just films praised by critics with advanced degrees in film studies at UCLA.

But the more we discuss our criteria, argue about them, and refine our opinions, the more we can arrive at better reasons for our criteria. In fact, this argument over criteria, or over our reasons for saying that, for example, a certain book is good or bad, is what makes the book review different from the high school book report. I value this thinking even when I talk with acquaintances over their assessment of a movie I am contemplating watching. I listen to hear not just, "It was a great movie," but also why they think it was great. Are they fans of this kind of movie? Do they value intense emotions, or thinking, or both? Can they tell the difference between thinking and feeling? Are they aware of the director's other work? In a very real way, what we are doing in a book review, movie review, performance review, or product review, is engaging in the formal features of the art of evaluation. The argument of evaluation will always consist of certain key parts. The following list is pretty reliable:

- Thesis, or the final evaluation of the thing in question.
- Specification of the thing in question, including background and comparison to other, similar things. (If it's a car, this will include ease of steering, torque, gas mileage, noise, and other factors. If it's a movie or a book, it will include a brief plot summary, list of main characters, the director's or the writer's or the main actor's other work, and comparisons to other products like it.)
- Statements of criteria.
- Evidence or support for the criteria, or demonstrations of how the thing in questions meets the criteria.
- Introduction.

These key parts of an evaluation do not all appear mechanically in the order given. They come up as they are important. But all of them will revolve around whatever the writer considers to be the main criteria, which will be made fairly plain and include the fact that the writer doesn't like sentimental scenes that "go over the top." A reviewer of a new romantic comedy may value it for the warm, hopeful feelings it inspires, for the chemistry of the leads, or she may criticize the obvious sexism that is often evident in this kind of movie. The fact that the criteria are subjective can be seen plainly in that the movies praised by film critics, who have often been through film school, are not the movies that many viewers, who seek two hours of entertainment or escape, want to see.

Consider the question of Nicholson's acting. If we were to question whether he is a great actor, we could base our reasoning on some of the following I've heard people use. First, is he or has he ever been a Shakespearean actor? People claim that the greatest actors have acted in the great bard's plays. Does this fit our criteria for a great actor, and did Nicholson ever do this? Second, has the actor ever been nominated for an Academy Award? Notice that this, like the previous value about being a Shakespearean actor, could be argued against. Third, we might look at the many roles Nicholson has been cast in and ask what these roles called for. Did he have to perform a range of emotions? Did he have to perform different kinds of characters? Or, in both questions, has he mainly played the same type of person and had the same emotions over and over again? We might also consider aspects of voice and physical presence and, certainly, the tendency to over-act.

The argument of evaluation, which places a focus on criteria, on why we do or do not value something, or on how well an aim is accomplished, is an important argument which will appear in every discipline. Historians argue over the best presidents, presumably with an eye to clarify for us certain characteristics that we value in democratically elected leaders. In education departments, teachers are evaluated for their ability to perform, and this is based on certain standards previously agreed upon. As well, educators have evaluated the effectiveness and soundness of government policies dealing with education. They will ask whether government officials really understand the difference between "teaching to the test" and creative and critical thinking. They will not hesitate to argue against policies put in place that lead to one kind of learning, memorizing facts, while the deeper learning prized by educational researchers is undermined.

We will evaluate performances of everything from sports teams, toasters, violins, and colleges, to public policies about immigration, new video games, and sports cars. The practice of evaluation is, obviously, an important one; it is a practice we may engage in that will help to clarify our thinking. Over the next week, it might be worth paying attention to the number of times a professor or a friend gives an evaluation or evaluative comments. Note whether you find yourself wanting them to provide some criteria for their judgment and, just as important, how often you or another asks for that criteria. Does it happen most often when you and another disagree on a judgment? ("No, I disagree; I think *Toy Story II* is a great kids' movie that grown-ups love.")

Evaluations are done for different reasons, depending on what is being evaluated. Some movies will be evaluated not only on technical grounds (acting, screenplay, directing, camera work) but also moral grounds. Many conservatives object to what they call gratuitous obscenities, sexual presentations, and violence.

feature 5.2

© Marten Czmanske, 2009. Used under license of Shutterstock, Inc.

The following assignment is designed to get you writing an evaluation.

Collect Two Reviews and Evaluate Them

Over the next week, collect two previously published evaluations. One should be of your favorite movie or book, and one should be taken from a field of your choice. Once you have them, highlight the reviews for the list of requirements discussed, especially focusing on the criteria the writer uses for the review. Notice what the reviewer seems to focus on the most. Is it criticisms of sentimentality? Or is it acting, or the script? Write a brief account of the review. To start, explain what you have always liked about the movie. Then list the reviewer's criteria. Then discuss whether that criteria is appropriate for the movie in question. Does it help you think more clearly about why you have responded to the movie in the way you have? Answer these questions and be prepared to defend them in a class discussion. Open yourself to further thinking about the issues that are raised.

Group Discussion

When you come to class, first read over at least two evaluations your classmates have brought in, and look over what they've written about them. Discuss your responses to the reviews.

Next, as a class, read one of the reviews of your classmates. Note and highlight the aspects of the review. Note the choices the writer makes and why. How many of his criteria do you agree with? How many of them do you disagree with because you are not the same gender? A different race or religion? No religion at all? How many of them simply don't matter to you because you are apathetic? Note how often you react with apathy.

After you have had the chance to think over writing this kind of argument and have read a number of different examples of it, try your hand at writing your own evaluation of a book you've read recently, a movie you've seen but have questions about, or a play you've seen.

Writing Your Essay: What Is "What You Know"?

Opinions matter in writing, as long as they are supported with persuasive evidence. One way of writing about opinion, as given above, is the argument that has evaluation itself as its focus. This argument is important because it helps us to clarify why we like something at the same time that it helps us to think about why we like it.

feature 5.3

© Alphonse Tran, 2009. Used under license of Shutterstock, Inc.

Another genre that involves opinion is the opinion essay we find in newspapers and in magazines, as well as in Internet spaces like blogs and Web sites. Opinion essays, when found in newspapers and on Web sites, are often concerned with policy and political issues. They involve strong opinions on one or another side of an issue.

Perhaps for many of us to this point, we've been taught to think that a topic for writing begins in what we know. This training has led us to reflect inwardly, like fiction writers or poets. But invention is not only about the "inward turn." As with the ancient Greeks, it also concerns the outward look—at others, at our communities, and at potential for the future. Most good writing does not stay on the inward turn for very long. After all, we are not self-authored individuals who spring to life without any help. Each of us is deeply tied to others, to perhaps many different communities. If you doubt this, consider every area of life that concerns you in any way, and think about how much of your thinking and decision making comes from the voices of others. Consider how many of your "individual convictions" are really commonplaces, with their sources in the communities you are part of.

In case you are having trouble thinking about what a commonplace is, consider the following examples. First, here's an idea I often hear now that is behind the growing divorce rate today: "Marriage is all about my happiness. If I am not happy, then it is my right to divorce him (or her) and find someone who makes me happy." The plots of many movies hang on this opinion.

This might seem to be true as a matter of course. But consider it again. Is it true? What might be some arguments against it? Consider that this commonplace, not often recognized as one, is behind the thinking of many young people today entering marriage. It is a very different belief about marriage than those held by previous generations. Though how marriage works may seem to be a settled issue, in fact there is much to argue and much to research about it.

It is possible to notice how plots for the movies often work around commonplace notions. There is a rare time when a movie will go against widely held social commonplaces or convictions. This is because they are designed to invite our participation, our assent. Note also that this commonplace, "If he (or she) doesn't make me happy, it is my right to seek a divorce so that I can find someone who does," forms an intersection between what we might call personal concerns and community concerns. Some will consider this a matter of fact. It is certainly a valuable place to start when thinking about commonly held opinions.

Consider a related commonplace: "The most important thing, the only thing that matters, is my own happiness." Is this true? What are the consequences of thinking this way? Is personal happiness more important than the happiness of others? Is my happiness right now, at this moment, more important than learning something that will later be important? (In this last one, I've actually paired one commonplace against the other) What are the consequences of not thinking this way? For purposes of invention, we might outline how each argument might unfold. Talk to others about it.

Here is another: "If you praise students and enhance their self-esteem, they will become smarter, more confident individuals." In fact, there is evidence that this commonplace, a centerpiece of the self-esteem movement in education, results in higher rates of narcissism. Research on the subject has led to the conclusion that enhancing self-esteem does not lead to better mastery of subject material. It does not lead to better math or writing ability. It does lead to the enhanced sense of entitlement. It just doesn't make us smarter than we would have been without it.

So far, the reaction might be that the commonplaces I've listed aren't really commonplaces but facts, truths, or pieces of wisdom. This reaction would be understandable, since it is most difficult to recognize our own assumptions as assumptions. But that is the point. Commonplaces, what ancient rhetoricians would have started with in their speaking and writing, are important, and we have good reasons for questioning them. The point is that they can and should be questioned. They may simply stand as self-evident, as obvious to us. We will only notice them as peculiar when someone else who does not agree with them forces the light on them and we begin to notice how they are notions deeply rooted in community assumptions.

In any case, it should be clear that examining deeply held convictions might lead us to research we might do to build support for or challenge our own ideas.

Perhaps we might start by thinking about what we know, as this also might cause us to move to what we don't know. If we are honest, it may be a short journey from what we know to what we don't know. We might want to read more, talk more to others, find out how our topic is situated in our own lives and in the lives of others around us. How much do we know about what we think we know? One area we might consider even though it doesn't seem like knowledge or a subject we ourselves own, is where the ancients began, in the commonplace. Think about a subject that matters to you, and then write down or think about some of the most common and even trite opinions or sayings that are made about it. These are not, finally, going to be your opinion or position, certainly. But knowing that they are social commonplaces, the points where many other people around us begin to think about the question, we can think about them. What might we argue to the contrary? How much of the commonplace is based on evidence?

In thinking about commonplaces to write about, consider an issue that matters to you and to others. Does it concern how you were educated? Does it concern your working life? Your political affiliations? Does it concern where you practice worship? Does it concern where you hang out? Choose an issue about which there are divided opinions, and begin thinking and writing about it. For your essay, you will be required to find out the opinions of your parents and siblings. Interview them. Find out what they think. Consider their opinions on the matter. Be prepared to incorporate this as part of your thinking. Include also some reading on the issue. Construct your argument and prepare to get feedback in class.

Consider the following commonplaces as examples. In class, add to this list. Consider that each one might be the cause of a spinoff to others. Consider this listing a start toward an essay. Think about different areas of life.

To get a good job, you need to first get a good education.
Don't be so heavenly-minded that you are no earthly good.
If you are over thirty, you can't possibly understand that struggles today's youth face.
All religious people are hypocrites.
Atheists have no reason to be moral.
In all things, practice moderation.
There's no need for government investment: let the marketplace dictate our culture. Only the marketplace determines what is valuable or worth doing. (See Ken Burns, "Standing Up for Public Television.")
Cheaters never prosper
A free market is best for business when it remains unregulated.
Character matters more than ability.
Healthy people never get depressed.
Playing Mozart for your unborn child will make her smarter.
Wealth is a sign of heavenly favor.
Genius stands outside of the community.
To prosper, all you need to do is work hard.
It's not what you know, it's who you know.

Consider also the following commonplaces sometimes addressed in this book:

Business majors (or science majors, or education majors) don't need to be good writers.
Everyone has his/her own writing style, and you can't criticize that.
You can't teach people to write well.

Crowley and Hawhee add the following:

Anyone can become president of the United States.
All men are created equal.
Everyone has a right to express his or her beliefs because free speech is protected by the Constitution. (21)

In their commentary on what they call these "widely accepted" common-places "in American discourse," Crowley and Hawhee note that there is a social construction to them, and "outside the communities that subscribe to them, commonplaces may be controversial" (21).

Crowley and Hahee underscore that commonplaces are the statements that go into and reflect one's ideology. "These beliefs are 'common,'" they write, "not because they are cheap or trivial but because they are shared 'in common' by many people." They suggest that when commonplaces are "contested," this leads to "issues in rhetoric, and it is the point of rhetoric to help people examine and perhaps to achieve agreement about issues" (20, 21).

It appears that we certainly can question opinions and formulate objections. This would seem to be in our own best interests.

Writing the Opinion Essay

For the following assignment, prepare to write an opinion essay of three to four pages that gives good reasons for holding an opinion that is different from others and swims against the current of popular thought. Or in three to four pages, give remarkable reasons why the tried and true commonplace is or is not a good idea.

To start, find and read an opinion essay in the local paper or on the Internet. Note the choices the writer makes. Does it begin with or, at some early point in the essay, assert a commonplace? As one example, consider that TV viewing is often blamed for poor reading scores and failing writing ability. This is a long-held notion, and before it, radio was blamed for poor literacy among high school and college students. In a 1930s *College English* article, a professor of English noted that it was common knowledge that "today's students" can't write because of radio crooners. Of course, today we recognize that the generation that grew up listening to Bing Crosby, Frank Sinatra, and those other silver-throated songbirds is responsible for buying most of the books in America today.

That TV is behind declines in literacy today is an unproven, though deeply held commonplace, a widespread belief, and it may be tied to reactionary fears about technology. Similar arguments are being marshaled today about the negative effects of computer games, Internet chat rooms, and texting on student writing and reading. Consider these suggestions and write an opinion essay arguing against the idea that the TV causes poor literacy rates. Or consider an argument that might also include today's computer technology.

Writing

Consider the role that a writer's *ethos* plays in whether we believe him or her. Focus your own concern on TV or on computers and video gaming. Consider whether or not your experience helps your *ethos*.

feature 5.5   Writing Prompt Reflection

Respond to Writing Prompt 5 at the beginning of this chapter—and the main points of this chapter concerning fact and opinion—by writing a commentary to it. Or write an essay in which you argue what you believe is the case concerning fact and opinion.

Grammar Interlude 5: Direct Objects

DIRECT OBJECTS

Nouns play different roles in sentences. The first role you've already discussed—the subject of the sentence. Another role nouns play can occur later in the sentence, after the verb, when they serve as the object of the verb's action. Consider the plural noun "ducks" and the proper noun "Bert" in the following two sentences:

Bert fed the ducks.   The ducks bit Bert.

- In the first sentence, "Bert" is the subject. "Ducks," being fed by Bert, are the direct object.
- In the second sentence, "Bert," pushed back behind the verb, is the direct object, and "ducks" is the subject.

This is the direct object. Some verbs, called transitive, need direct objects to be receivers of the action. Direct objects are sometimes called predicate nouns, because they are nouns that are found in the predicate—the predicate is the verb part of the sentence.

Ex. 1. The following sentences all have direct objects. First, underline the direct object in each. Then, in each, draw a line separating the subject from the predicate.

1. The student flunked the test.
2. The role player fed coins into the slot machine
3. The reader finished the book.
4. The reader liked the book.
5. The reader loved the book.
6. The reader hated the book.

Ex. 2. Some of the following sentences have direct objects, and some don't. Put an X by those sentences that have direct objects.

_____ 1. In the late summer of that year, we built a house.
_____ 2. By the time we arrived at the museum, Cynthia had gone home.
_____ 3. We don't have time for this discussion.
_____ 4. When you wake up, I will have moved to Boston
_____ 5. When you wake up, I will have moved Boston.

____ 6. The time is now for all good men and women to come to the aid of their country.

____ 7. The bird ate the worm in the grass.

DISCUSSION

What do you notice about the sentences that do not have direct objects? What kind of verbs work in those sentences? What other kinds of words are in those sentences?

Ex. 3. Look at a paragraph from the final draft of your last essay. Write down the number of sentences that have the subject-verb-object pattern. How often do they appear?

QUESTIONS FOR REFLECTION AND PRACTICE

What knowledge did you gain here?

Do these routines teach you anything of value for your own writing?

If so, what?

What will you do to connect with your future style and editing choices?

Chapter *Six*

Inquiry, Invention, and Research

Chapter Overview

This chapter outlines what college-level research does and how it unfolds. First, research writing is not simply impersonal, objective, or exclusively focused on facts. Rather, good research can begin with a question or some issue of importance to a writer or a writer's community. When that community is a college one, certain expectations about method must be observed. A model for research is suggested which combines both the writer's opinions and framework and the integration of primary and secondary sources. Following this, the section on how to skillfully integrate sources through direct quote, paraphrase, and summary demonstrates how to develop an authoritative voice for research.

Inquiry and Questions

Inquiry starts with questions we really want answered. Some questions are best addressed in specific disciplines, like biology. A cure for cancer, for example, or questioning why men have facial hair, would lead to a method and line of inquiry that includes the scientific method. Questions into different opinions regarding poverty might involve us in economic theory. Wanting to answer our questions might lead to areas where others have investigated. Certainly, we might find ourselves reading or "re-searching" what others have already searched for and published.

But questions arise. How much of our search can be shaped by our reading? Should we conduct interviews with people? Should we write a survey and distribute it to people? How do we learn what we need to know? Inquiry has to do with a method. Inquiry will be our starting point. At the beginning of a project, invention is an important part of the process. Invention will concern reflection, brainstorming, and reading.

For many, learning to write has come as the result of a long series of tasks over many years. From your most recent courses, you've had experiences that

feature 6.1   Writing Prompt 6

"Inquiring Minds Want to Know" and What TV Does to Certain Ideas

A TV advertisement for The National Inquirer, a gossip magazine sold at the checkout lanes of most grocery stores, used to repeat the slogan, "Inquiring minds want to know." By connecting a quality with a product and repeating the product's name in a catchy phrase, this was advertising at its best. Less often remarked on, though, was the question of whether this ad also made fun of the idea of inquiry, since the magazine's pages were filled with dubious gossip about celebrities, recent sightings of UFO's, new findings about the emergence of the Antichrist, amazing predictions by Nostradamus, and accounts of two-headed babies who did higher-level math. Connecting the idea of inquiry with obviously contrived, salacious gossip and the freakish aspects of nature, these ads suggested that the consumer's basest, most outlandish preoccupations, were really forms of engaging in inquiry.

In contrast, inquiry challenges the status quo, the usual way of thinking about an issue. It constitutes something other than reading gossip, which usually does little more than reinforce social values already in place, or being morbidly curious about freakishness, which also serves to reinforce the norm. Inquiry involves curiosity, what most children display almost simply by nature. This curiosity can come in different ways at different ages, but it can be about real issues that matter to us, problems that bother us, thinking that seems to result in paradox. Methods for inquiry may start with something as simple as read-ing—blogs, newspapers, books, magazines.

However, the process doesn't work the way that it is often practiced in high school, or even in many of our classes in college, where students are taught to collect "facts" or "quotes" from the library or the Internet and then arrange these in a paper. This is not really inquiry either. When we are seeking quotable lines and "facts" to support our own view, we are not doing inquiry. We are starting with and staying with what we already know and skipping over the real questions in our subject area. In contrast, the kind of research worth doing is that which changes us. We change our minds as we learn more.

feature 6.2   Library Sign

© JJJ, 2009. Used under license from Shutterstock, Inc.

have shaped how you represent to yourself the task of writing–whether any planning is needed before you write, whether writing requires your thinking, whether "good" writing is really just subjective and a teacher's personal opinion. Though the journey has been your own solitary struggle, some things that have happened to you have been predictable. For most of us, writing instruction has involved learning to write reports and use sources for those reports. We've been taught the five-paragraph theme but little about the real genres that writers and readers employ. We've been taught a few mechanical lessons in what to do as "prewriting," but little of this has been connected with real inquiry into issues.

And the research tradition we've been taught has followed a fairly standard regimen, one that has presented a few important, controversial, and not necessarily valuable lessons about what knowledge is, what facts are, and what value opinions have.

Consider the following.

The Formula: Researching Facts

Some questions are easily answered.

Even in the third grade, when we were first introduced to encyclopedias and dictionaries, we learned that if we wanted to know (a) how many yards are in a mile or (b) who served as our thirty-fourth president, we could either (a) do the math on it or (b) look it up. Finding our answer, we reached the end of our search. Some of us may have thought silently about where the random measurements "yard" and "foot" came from. Furthermore, did both mean the same length in the 17th century, and did the second ever have anything to do with the human foot? We may have questioned this even if we didn't raise these as issues for our teachers. We certainly might have questioned the basis for our certainty in this matter. Some may have thought about how to apply this new knowledge of yards and feet to the local terrain. But most of us were content to leave it at the answer we found. We thought about it no more.

A little later, we were taught to select a topic, say bottlenose dolphins, and go on the Internet and read facts about them. After we'd compiled enough facts, we then organized them into a report, which was basically what the Internet tells us about this particular dolphin. If our teacher was conscientious, she also taught us to provide citations for the sources of our information, even when we paraphrased it.

Some people approach all knowledge in this way, thinking of it as "research," as already formed knowledge to look for, a set of inert facts collected in a book somewhere or a Web site that someone else has compiled. We simply look them up. We find the right book or, more recently perhaps, the right Web site, to have our questions answered. Our "finger-tip" fact file and our book of quotable quotes may have changed due to technological advances, certainly, but we are still approaching knowledge from the same bias, as something that has to do with "filling in the blank," as on a test. However, some of us have not taken our thinking about why we do research or how to do it much further than this fifth grade model of research, which can be stated in the following formula: Select your topic, find facts, and report them. *early writing model*

This view of research is simple. It is also very different from the research that is esteemed in most academic departments of universities. Research as first taught in the fourth or fifth grade almost assumes that the knower is getting ready to be a contestant on a game show, like the popular television game show *Jeopardy*. But for most academics, research must go beyond discrete facts.

goal: generating new knowledge

Research A: High School Objectivity

What is presented in most high school English courses of research shows the influence of teaching about "objectivity," mostly concerned with learning about what is done in the sciences. This training, usually presented in absolute terms that are tied to grades, requires first that the writer avoid, at all costs to objectivity, the use of the first person "I." (Some teachers also include prohibitions against the second person "you".) It also requires that the writer purge her writing of her own opinions. Only the "facts on file" are necessary. Nothing of a human voice or community should darken the pages of good research. Many textbooks are written in this desired, "objective" voice.

Yet simply purging a paper of "I" will not make the writing "objective." After all, you will still be focusing on certain ideas and omitting others. These focuses and omissions are subjective choices we all make, and they should probably simply be acknowledged as unavoidable.   *goal: transperancies of our biases*

The best research is almost always done with a strong agenda in mind—finding a cure for AIDS, say, or figuring out new ways of reducing greenhouse gases. These show serious commitments, not objectivity. Research may consist of addressing a question for a class, but this doesn't have to mean purging your humanity. This also doesn't mean a return to peppering your papers with all of those "In my opinion," "I believe that," and "I think that" phrases. Obviously, your high school teacher was right to object to the statement, "In my opinion, the military draft was wrong," simply because the first part, "In my opinion," is wordy and unnecessary. This is obviously your opinion, and your saying so undermines it, draws needless attention to the fact that it is opinion, and may even cause the reader to ask, "And who do you think you are?" Cut that part out. Restating it as "The military draft was wrong" does not make it suddenly objective. It is still your opinion. It is just worded better. What I am suggesting is not that you should allow all of those "In my opinion" and "I believe that" phrases back into your paper. Rather, recognize that you are still dealing with opinion, even stating it better following your high school teacher's logic.

Research for College Courses

Fact-finding and the chimera of high school objectivity described above are not what we mean by research or by inquiry. It is not something that is easily answered by looking it up in a book. It is not a lab report, though some disciplines at the university require you to write a report of your lab study. And instead of reaching for objectivity by omitting pronouns, we admit to certain unavoidable and even valued connections to community, gender, and ethnicity. But we also aim for fairness, balance, reasonableness, and even, if possible, disinterestedness.

Certainly, where our worst biases prevent us from being fair, we should be honest about them. By research, then, we mean something more human, larger, and more complicated than high school "objectivity."

In contrast to the perspectives given above, college research writing involves joining an academic community, understanding the kinds of knowledge it values, and writing well in the genres it values. When we have decided on a topic to write on, this will involve finding out what has already been done with a subject that is of interest to that community and working with it, sometimes giving it new perspectives. It involves knowing how the community documents sources, certainly, but also reading sources deeply and responding critically to those sources.

key paragraph ★

Writing, Research, and Community

Considering that writing is more than finding facts and reporting them, we might also claim that connections to a community constitute the beginnings of writing, thinking, and research. Your experiences as a young woman or man count for beginning, primary research and questions. Consider that your research might begin with the very concerns of where you reside. What questions most concern you right now? What questions most concern your parents, your neighbors, your fellow synagogue-, mosque-, or church-goers? What issues arise for you as a beginning college student in a new community? In the interest of openness and fairness, consider the following research model.

One Research Model

use real ?s
~~out~~ to address
a community

1. As already noted, research usually begins with real questions, often with questions that are of concern to a community. If your community is an academic discipline, what are the concerns you are hearing about? Address them in the way that the community expects to be addressed.

2. All research can also start with and include experiences or evidence from our own life. But using personal experience is tricky simply because it is too easy to overgeneralize from it or ignore evidence to the contrary. In response to a personal account, the question can always be raised, "But wasn't that just your experience?" One way that writers often support personal experiences is by including interviews with others who have had similar experiences, surveys they design to focus on certain responses, and extensive reading from others who have thought and even theorized about the experiences in question.

An example might help demonstrate how this works. One person I know decided as a ninth grader to see what would happen if he enrolled in "basic" English instead of "honors," which he had been accepted into. As predicted, in basic English, he was treated as unqualified, as a basic writer. Though he'd placed second in a short story contest the year before in the eighth grade, in high school his ninth grade "basic" English instructor assumed he was plagiarizing when he handed in a poem she considered to be "too good for anyone in the class." Of course, the problem with this person's experiment is the experience that followed it. He was stuck in the "basic" track throughout high school. This led to his second discovery. In his experience, he found that no one went back to check on the files to see that he had been wrongly placed in his English class. High school counselors are busy people, with hundreds, even thousands of students to track. He was stuck. But he learned from this two things: First, in his case, expectations shaped his teacher's perceptions of how her students would perform in basic English; and second, at his high school, at least, mistakes were hard to rectify.

But the question remains: How should my friend use this personal experience? It would be overgeneralizing to say that this happens in every case. Indeed, some counselors at some high schools are more detailed than this, and some high school English teachers are not as jaded as his was. What he should do with these experiences is use them as the basis for his research questions. Start with these: Do high school teachers' expectations shape how they respond to and read their students' work? And do all high school counselors treat their students as mere numbers?

To start, these questions might be addressed by conducting interviews with others. What were their experiences in high school basic English? This might be further supported by taking a survey, using pointed questions, and getting as many samples as possible. Survey data can often prove useful as evidence to support broad trends.

This should demonstrate that even personal experiences can be considered research, especially when we learn something from them about questions we can raise that might answer or challenge other research.

3. All research is deepened, made more authoritative, changed, refined, confirmed, and opened by drawing on other sources than our own experience for evidence in our research. This includes interviews, surveys, and studies that other people, specialists, have conducted. It also includes other first person accounts and books of research that others have compiled to add to our understanding of historical situations. Most of our high school training concerned this kind of research. Along with our own research in terms of interviews and surveys and even experiences, these secondary sources need to be documented.

4. All research becomes a thoughtful construction of an argument. It shares in the making of knowledge for a community. It answers the "so what" question

for all writing so that it isn't simply an empty exercise in getting on *Jeopardy*. It also becomes a narrative of our search for answers and why they might be important to others.

Research Starts with the Right Questions

To start, reframe your initial thinking about your topic as a question. To find this question, begin with your convictions, your assumptions on the topic right now. Find out how your topic is affecting the people you know. For example, if you are convinced that television viewing among children leads to violence, write this conviction down on a sheet of paper. Follow this by rephrasing it as a question: does television viewing among children lead to violence? Now that you have your belief phrased as a question, you will want to begin addressing it. Try to think about variations on the question. For example, "How much television viewing is harmful to children's sense of values?"

Or consider the question of health care. What is the best way to cut down on health care costs? This is a huge question, but as you begin to research, you may see that the need to explore many different avenues of thought and put things together, construct them, actually leads you to a narrower question. Consider the question a student raised several years ago. This question constituted the start of his research. He began by announcing that "the *Los Angeles Times* is a liberal newspaper and against the pro-life perspective." At the start, this was his conviction, probably based on talking with his family and his friends. To get

feature 6.3   Typewriter

© Kerry Garvey, 2009. Used under license from Shutterstock, Inc.

started, he saw his research as mainly consisting of going back and reading all that the paper covered on abortion over a certain time span. Another question we raised had to do with definitions of "bias." What were we looking for? What would be "fair" coverage of this issue? As my student compiled his research, what he actually found was nuanced. He found that the *Times* had actually been criticized for bias on the abortion issue in the early 1990s, but they had also responded to these criticisms by trying to be more fair. In his own estimation, my student's final paper reflected how one major newspaper had responded to accusations of bias. This was a fine research essay, not the least because it was fair and honest. It was also effective because it began with the writer's own concerns and biases as he tried to find answers.

Granted, some of his research consisted of looking things up, but all of his questions were not answered on a single page. Instead, as is more often the case than not, our quest for knowledge will require our own active participation, a certain amount of connecting dots, of adding one idea to another, of getting hints, of challenging assumptions. The research we do that is worthwhile will be constructed in part as we grow and examine our own assumptions about a question or an issue and in part as we examine the assumptions and beliefs expressed in some of the works we read in our research. As we learn more, we may find ourselves questioning what we previously thought before coming into a new and better sense of a larger perspective on things. All opinions are certainly open to question. Whether we are concerned with understanding a reasonable, ethical position to take on an issue, such as health care, the best federal policies to avoid a prolonged recession, or the most reasonable explanation for the rise of hate policies toward Jews in Hitler's Third Reich, we are at a new threshold of understanding, not simply trying to reconfirm old prejudices. Our work will require of us questions and creativity in addition to learning to properly footnote our ideas, avoid plagiarism, and write according to guidelines.

Primary and Secondary Research

In the discussion of this model for research, I have placed importance on personal research by stating its use first, before library research. I do this because I am aware of the deadening stereotype of the academic research paper that consists of looking up sources in the library or on the Internet, and I want to broaden this perspective. Research, indeed, any writing we do that is worth our time, does begin with our identities in various ways. Obviously women and men will have different concerns and even a different take on the importance of any number of things, from child day care programs, to education, to sports, to health care concerns. Just as obviously, race, ethnicity, social class, and income will define many issues for us, as will our religious perspectives and commitments. None of these concerns needs to be discounted, but we do need to understand how to draw on them and integrate them with secondary sources and make them persuasive for the academic communities for which we are writing. It remains true that drawing on sources for evidence gives writing authority, but it will depend how we integrate this material.

Primary Sources

Primary research involves reading and quoting from a first, originating source, whether it is a creative work or a scientific study, rather than reading about that source through other commentators. Here are a few simple examples. A primary source is a novel by Mark Twain. The secondary source will be criticism of or commentary on that novel. A primary source might be a journal entry by Benjamin Franklin, whereas a secondary source will be a commentary that quotes from or draws on that source in some way. Be able to recognize when you are getting a comment on something and not the thing itself. When you encounter someone quoting someone else, ask "Did Mark Twain (or Ben Franklin) really say that? Let's go back to the source." Usually, the context of the source is quite different from the new context it is being quoted in.

Be aware of bias in your secondary sources as well.

And take note: you may think that your teacher is only interested in how well you use the MLA documentation system for your paper, or the fact that you get enough sources for your paper and meet the required page length. It is more likely that these concerns of your teacher have to do with a deeper concern than "pickiness" or grammatical correctness. They more likely have to do with your writing in a way that you have authority with your audience and don't sound like someone who can't even get documentation right, which will cast a poorer light on your ideas than you think. In fact, getting your citations right, whether in the APA or the MLA system, reflects on your authority as a writer, on your *ethos*. The people you want reading your paper should be able to focus on your ideas, not on your failure with something considered so rudimentary as documentation (or grammar). Your failure to document sources correctly will lead your reader to suspect that you've gotten other things wrong in your paper. Perhaps you have even plagiarized.

If you think this is picky, consider how you felt the last time you walked into a car dealership. Was the person there who greeted you well-dressed, or did he wear boots made of snake skin? And did he pay attention to details? Or was he sloppy and offered you a chair to sit in that had grease stains on it? How did being invited to sit in a chair like that make you feel about buying a car from him?

Consider that the grease stain on the chair looks just like those misspelled words or that sloppiness with documentation in a paper. The message from these missed details is clear: you didn't really pay attention to what you were doing.

Other Voices: Joining the Conversation

Writers respond to the ideas of others. No one is the "original author," the first ever to speak on all subjects.

Everyone who is born, everyone who goes to college, every scholar, everyone who writes, and everyone who does research, begins by getting ideas that come from other people, from the culture in which they are tutored and raised. To repeat, this includes scholars and academics. Scholars who write for an academic audience, writing for their peers in academic research journals to report new findings and new research, may be the proud owners of awards that claim originality. But a more accurate rendering of this picture—and it is a picture that is being asserted more and more often—is that this aspect of research begins in a community. It never just springs as new and never thought before. It is often drawn from the thinking of others. For example, many of the psychoanalyst Carl Jung's depictions of the human consciousness, unconscious, and what he came to term the "collective unconscious," came from his work with Sigmund Freud. It is no matter that he frequently differed with Freud in his writing and often criticized him. The very presence of this criticism shows that he was responding to his mentor and colleague, and that, in fact, many of his ideas might be traced to Freud. And the same might be said of Freud, that he was responding not only to his own original research, but to the ideas of his colleagues as he entered the field in which he worked.

When we begin to write, we will find it necessary to use sources in two ways. One way is as the voices against which or with which we are writing, as the voices representing the current view on our topic as we come to it. That is, as Jung did with Freud, we will want to cite our authors before we refute them or agree with them. The second way we will want to use resources is to thoughtfully and carefully draw on good research that has been done to support our ideas. In both of these ways, we show that we are joining a conversation in an informed way. Even if we are then writing about something as common to first year writing as gun control, we are doing it in an informed way—we know what has been and is being said about our topic, we know the present context of our arguments (whether there has been another school shooting, for example), and we know how this context will include our own ideas and our research.

Since using sources, that is, the voices and ideas of others, and not just facts or dumped quotes, is necessary to our research task, we must do it well.

Three Ways to Gain Authority for Writing by Including Sources in Your Writing

Using sources well matters because it is important to academic readers. It can enhance your authority with the audience that matters to you. Although a poor performance here can look like grease stains on the paper, detracting from your writing and ideas, it can, more devastatingly, in the worse case, lead to plagiarism. Many colleges and universities are beginning to respond to academic cheating with a "gotcha" mentality, "taking prisoners," so to speak, and prosecuting to the full extent of the law. Many are resorting to Turnitin.com, a computer Web site that automatically downloads student papers and compares them to hundreds of thousands of other papers and documents, looking for any part of a paper that has been taken from another source and not clearly documented. The result is instantaneous. Anything you've copied into your paper without correctly documenting will appear in a sickly green color. But even if your school or teacher doesn't resort to Turnitin.com, it is still possible to detect an act of deliberate stealing.

If you are caught, the consequences for plagiarism could run a gamut from a failing grade on the offending paper, to failing the course in which you plagiarized, to being expelled from the school where you did it. The last consequence, in most cases, comes after a second or third published offense, but you want to avoid any of these outcomes.

What is plagiarism? It occurs when you pass off the words and ideas of other people, in part or in whole, as your own work. Simply put, if you'd given a footnote or a parenthetical reference and a works cited page for these quotes, you'd have been an outstanding researcher. But instead, plagiarism occurs when you take someone else's ideas about bottlenose dolphins, put them in your own words (this is called paraphrase), and fail to document that they are someone else's ideas. Plagiarism also occurs when you take the exact words of another source and put them in your own writing and fail to provide quotation marks and documentation to show that it belongs to someone else. Finally, plagiarism occurs when you take someone else's paper and submit it as your own.

The way to avoid these scenarios is to be honest, obviously. Don't buy someone else's paper and submit it as your own work. But also, master the following three ways to include sources in your writing. Using these three ways skillfully—using direct quotes, paraphrasing ideas, and summarizing—will build authority into your writing.

Using Direct Quotes

The first, most obvious, way to use material from another source is to quote directly from it. We do this when we use, word for word, the very sentences composed by another—whether the word of an author, a speaker, a person on a Web site, words in a pamphlet, a letter to an editor, or a federal law. When we quote the exact words of others like this, we need to first make sure that every part of what they've said or written is bounded by quotation marks, one at the beginning of their passage, and one at the end. This should look like the following example:

"We are now in position to suggest that another factor in the choice of the generalized phrase was aesthetic distance."

Notice, however, that just putting the above passage in quotation marks is not enough. We still don't know who wrote the passage. We need the second part of quoting accurately, which is to include a footnote as a parenthetical reference after the quotation mark. This parenthetical reference should include the author's last name and the page number from which the quote is taken:

"We are now in position to suggest that another factor in the choice of the generalized phrase was aesthetic distance" (Weaver 175).

Notice that in the passage above, the parenthetical reference appears a space after the quotation mark, and the period is placed after it. This now accurately signals that the quoted sentence is from a writer named Weaver, and the reader, to know more, can go to the Works Cited page at the end of the paper and look up the source listed there for Weaver to find out more about it. Whether it is a book or a journal article or a Web site, what the work is titled, and when and where it was published—all of this information must appear on the Works Cited page.

The third part of a competent use of quotations is known as the "signal phrase," such as the following:

According to one author,
In the words of Jane Austen,
As one scholar suggests,
As Carl Jung puts it,

These signal phrases are just four examples of an endless variation on the conversational tag theme known in fiction writing circles as "he said, she said." Like the use of the conversational tag in fiction—as in the following, "Is this, then, goodbye?" she asked—the signal phrase announces the voices of others in your writing. Unlike the use of the conversational tag in fiction, the signal phrase in research writing appears not at the end but at the beginning of the quote, just before a quotation. It provides a smooth transition between your own writing and the language of the quotation you are using. For this reason, it is a good stylistic device. But it also serves a function of setting up a boundary and signaling to your reader that someone else's voice is about to be heard. If we think of our research in the terms spelled out by Kenneth Burke in the chapter on rhetoric, we will understand that we are joining a conversation, and that in order to make our own voice heard, we need to place it in context with other voices, with what has been said before our arrival in the "parlor room," or area of our research. For example, consider the quote from Weaver in this new context.

Many people react the same way when they hear or read speeches from earlier centuries. The sound of the words come off as pompous or bombastic, especially with the large phrases that invoke God or country or history. But this wasn't necessarily the case when the speeches were given. The real reason could have been that "the choice of the generalized phrase was aesthetic distance" (Weaver 175).

This is okay as an example of incorporating a quotation. The quotation marks clearly signal the quote, and the writer's name and the page number for the quoted words appear in the parenthetical reference. Best, however, would be to do the following:

Many people react the same way when they hear or read speeches from earlier centuries. The sound of the words come off as pompous or bombastic, especially with the large phrases that invoke God or country or history. But this wasn't necessarily the case when the speeches were given. As Richard Weaver suggests, "another factor in the choice of the generalized phrase was aesthetic distance" (175).

The signal phrase, highlighted above, is an important piece of this "parlor room" practice. Though the quotation marks clearly signal the boundary between quoted words and your own, the signal phrase provides a sleek, valuable transition that guides your reader. Without it, the quote you use will feel "dumped" randomly into the paper.

Paraphrasing Others' Voices

The signal phrase is especially important to the practice of paraphrase, the second way of incorporating source material—everything from evidence, to other arguments, other theories—into your own writing. Like the direct quote, the paraphrase usually concerns just one passage, or perhaps explaining one or two ideas in another writer's work. But unlike the quote, the paraphrase happens when you put that passage or set of ideas in your own words, rewording it to your own style.

When you reword the passage in question, you do not need to include quotation marks, except for those words that you do quote directly from the author. But you absolutely must provide a parenthetical documentation, connecting your paraphrased passage with the actual page in the author's writing. If you do not, you are guilty, whether or not you intend plagiarism.

Also needed, to mark a boundary between your ideas, your writing, and that of your source, is the signal phrase. This is especially needed now that the quote marks aren't used, as they are in the direct quote. Now, without the signal phrase, there is no way to indicate to your reader that you are peddling someone else's ideas. Please use it. For example, look at the paraphrase of the Weaver passage here:

It is Richard Weaver's suggestion that one reason 19th-century orators used "the generalized phrase," a term he gives to phrases that create historical context to a speech, like "the march of history," or "echoing down the annals of time," was to create "aesthetic distance," something that provided a high stature for the speaker and a respectful consideration from the crowd who heard him (175).

Notice that the signal phrase starts this off, and for two key terms of Weaver's, "the generalized phrase" and "aesthetic distance," I've provided quotation marks. The other phrases I've quoted are not in his text, but they are typical "general phrases" that might have been used in the 19th century. So I've set them off as coming from somewhere other than my own voice.

Notice also that because I've used Weaver's name in the signal phrase, I've not needed to put Weaver's name in the parenthetical reference. This is one variation on the parenthetical reference. If you include the name in the signal phrase, as I did above, only the page number is needed in the parenthetical documentation. On the other hand, if I had not included Weaver's name in the signal phrase—if I had done the following, the name would be needed in the parenthetical documentation:

It is one scholar's suggestion that one reason 19th century orators used "the generalized phrase," a term he gives to phrases that create historical context to a speech, like "the march of history," or "echoing down the annals of time," was to create "aesthetic distance," something that provided a high stature for the speaker and a respectful consideration from the crowd who heard him (Weaver 175).

An Unfortunate Paraphrase Example: On Not Using the Signal Phrase

Notice what happens in the following passage when the paraphrased material is not bounded by a signal phrase:

Many people react the same way when they hear or read speeches from earlier centuries. The words come off as pompous or bombastic, especially with the large phrases that invoke God or country or history. One reason 19th century orators may have used "the generalized phrase," a term for phrases that create historical context to a speech, like "the march of history," or "echoing down the annals of time," was to create "aesthetic distance," something that provided a high stature for the speaker and a respectful consideration from the crowd who heard him (Weaver 175).

This is an unfortunate example that happens frequently. Though the writer has signaled Weaver's ideas at the end of the passage, there is no clear indication of how much of the passage belongs to Weaver. Most of the paragraph has been passed off as the writer's own. A better way to paraphrase is to signal when your ideas end and another's begins.

When Do I Paraphrase? Quote?

When do you paraphrase and when do you quote?

· In most textbooks, the rule is to paraphrase most of the time and only quote directly from a passage when the quote is memorably said, better than you or anyone else could say it, or if it is typical of an argument you wish to refute. Or, of course, if the words of an opposing argument are especially provocative or insulting or helpful to your own argument, quote them.

Use paraphrase most of the time, and always announce paraphrases with signal phrases. Doing this demonstrates that you have understood the material you are incorporating in your text. It helps you avoid the appearance of being quote dependent, of being lazy, and of wanting to pad your paper, all of which result from an overuse of quotation.

Using Summary Writing to Report Your Research

A third way to include the words and ideas of others in your writing is to write summaries of their articles and arguments. A summary is a brief account of another's writing, a paragraph, or perhaps, for book summaries, a page or two in your own words. We summarize when we want to capture the whole of an argument or the whole of a thought in a book. We do this to support our own position in an argument. Or we do it to anticipate an argument we do not agree with. The same rule about signal phrases to introduce paraphrases holds for the summary. But because a summary concerns the whole of a piece, the page number is not needed, unless we have chosen to summarize a part of a larger, more complicated argument that does not apply to the context of our argument.

Summary writing allows us to capture a number of other arguments in a short space in our writing. It also allows us, if we are fair, to capture the thought of another, not just a quotation or two. The summary, to be effective, usually does not focus on great quotes or details. Nor does it stop to criticize the writing, though the writer may choose to do so after the summary is completed. In fact, one reason to write a summary is to then criticize the author. This is one of the main parts of the typical book or film review, which will include a partial plot or book summary in its critique. Mainly, though the summary gives the author's thesis or main point, followed by the main supporting points of the thought. The following is an example of Richard Weaver's argument, from which the above quotation about "aesthetic distance" was taken.

It is Richard Weaver's argument in "The Spaceousness of Old Rhetoric" that the 19th century orator, whose words are read today as peculiar and antique, once had the benefit of speaking to audiences who expected him to evoke great historical and geographical spaces in his speeches. What today are heard as bombastic phrases or terms we might in a court of law question or refute, Weaver argues were once heard as "uncontested terms" (166), terms that the speaker and audience could share and take for granted; in fact, it may have been that the hearers sought for these terms, which were not meant to "make them think" so much as to "remind them of what they already knew" (172). Weaver suggests that the appearance of these "uncontested terms" demonstrates that there has been a huge cultural change over the last hundred years or so, one in which we see a social consensus breaking down.

Notice that my summary includes little more than the main point of Weaver's article and his main subpoints, which include what he believes are the consequences of his thinking. Notice also that I included parenthetical references only for words actually quoted from Weaver's text. The works cited entry for Weaver's article will appear in alphabetical order on my works cited page, as follows:

Weaver, Richard. "The Spaceousness of Old Rhetoric." The Ethics of Rhetoric. Davis: Hermagoras, 1985: 164–185.

Gaining Authority for Writing

As you incorporate material from other sources in the three ways outlined above, you will not be "padding" your paper but giving it backbone, substance, and authority, especially if you use your documentation style competently. But something will have to happen before the writing of your first draft. Indeed, part of the problem with writing research will first involve a longer process in becoming proficient in your subject. Some writers don't get involved in long processes and might default to a mentality of "looking quotes or facts up", or to the high school idea described earlier in this chapter of rushing together a list of sources into a paper that is little more than a "brain dump" with no opinions in it and no thinking involved. If we do this, we will not be able to challenge our own assumptions about our ideas. We will not be able to think about the assumptions of others. We won't really think about the topic in any depth that allows us to grow in knowledge. Worst of all, we will not engage in what it means to do research at the college level. We aren't really "joining the conversation."

In contrast, you know you are enacting the real process if you find that you are actually reading material and coming up against your authors' biases. If you find yourself questioning a researcher's assumptions in an article you are reading, you are doing well. Because you are not just looking for facts but also for how those facts are being used, you can actually include in your writing and discussion something about the nature of your researchers' biases. You are starting to do the work of critical thinking. If you allow the process to continue and actually try to gain new information and insights, when you do begin to write you can do so with some authority on the subject. Part of the reason for doing research, then, is to earn the right to speak to others who share our interests, if not our perspective. We do this by finding out what research has been done on our topic. To do this, start with the books and articles you've already read and have on the subject. What names come up in those books and articles? Write these down and look for them in the library. Do any of the books or articles have a bibliography? Scan these and put check marks by all promising articles. The key at the start is to gain as many potential sources as possible.

Remember, you are not looking for simple quotes to dump into a paper you've already made up your mind about. You are looking to learn more about your subject so that you can justify having others listen to your opinions.

In addition to collecting facts, opinions, and theories from your reading, you will want to write down all of your opinions that may come to mind. But put these in your research notes or journal. Don't wait for your first draft to do this.

Some teachers suggest using note cards at this point in the process. Whether you do this, or use some other system to keep your sources straight, is up to you and your teacher. If you do use note cards, be sure to reserve some for jotting down, even roughly and half-formed, your own opinions. Certainly a notebook in which you can gather and even organize your research is worth your time. Be prepared to show your teacher your early work on this project. Once you have begun to read and learn more about your topic, it is time to ask if you know someone or can meet someone who can reasonably be termed an expert on the subject. Think about them as a possible source for an interview. From your reading, begin to compile a list of potential questions for this expert to answer.

Writing about Your Research: Interview Questions

One way to get an understanding of how your sources differ and are similar in their framing or perspective is to place them side by side and look at what each seems to say about similar issues. Note where they are the same and where they differ. Imagine how the writers of your articles might respond if they were asked certain questions. As your look over your sources, frame "interview questions" that you might ask. Asking the right questions is sometimes difficult because we must really tune in and listen to what others are saying, especially in a given context. This is true of how we try to hold political campaigns, though it does appear for many today that most races for office are usually treated like horse races, with mostly insults being exchanged rather than ideas and ideology.

For your research, however, your first writing about it can be facilitated in the following assignment, which calls for you to create a dialogue between three or four key perspectives on your issue in part one, followed by a second part in which you as moderator raise your own questions not addressed by your sources and take issue with the sources, giving your own opinions. In this dialogue and debriefing paper, in the first part, you must try to do what your high school teacher urged on you. You must try to be fair in presenting the different main "sides" to your issue, giving each a fair reading and calling, reserving your own ideas and opinions for the second part, in which you debrief your audience.

For this assignment, you are free to set it up in a talk show or radio show interview format, but be sure to give each side equal treatment, especially the position you most disagree with at the present writing. You can set this paper up as you might a play, starting with a brief set up of the scene, followed by dialogue lines labeled for each "character." The characters could be ones you make up, or they could be the writers you are reading who are most typical of the position in question. Also, you are to create a persona for yourself in this, someone to moderate the debate.

feature 6.4

© JJJ, 2009. Used under license from Shutterstock, Inc.

You should be creative with this, but do not let parody or the "persona" or the format aspect of this assignment become more important or take up more room than the critique and reading or your sources. For this assignment you must cite at least six of your sources, as the authors will want to cite the information, from themselves or other writers who agree or disagree with them. Make this a true dialogue between differing positions. Look for real agreement, disagreement.

Your paper should be at least five pages. You must accurately and successfully use MLA documentation, providing parenthetical references, signal phrases, and a works cited page.

Other Arguments to Research and Explore
Another Model

Another deeply held but unconfirmed assumption: "Today's young generation faces unbelievable pressures that previous generations could not have dreamed of."

This is said often by parents, young people, educators, and journalists. Is this assertion true? Or are we just more sensitive to what young people face than parents used to be? What does it mean? And how do we go about proving that this is the case, that students today face pressures that their parents could not have known? How could this statement be proved?

Recast this as a question: "Do many members of today's young generation face new pressures that previous generations did not?"

Then, in a project that you design, try to compile lists of things that are considered hard things that young people face, both now and in the past. To compile this list, talk to friends and peers about why they think their lives are so hard. Or perhaps you will find out that they don't think their lives are hard at all. At any rate, try to define what we mean by pressures people face. In addition to your lists, consult psychology texts that discuss stress and pressure and their effects. Do what these texts outline fall into place alongside what you hear people saying? And as for the lists you are compiling, does the pressure you are hearing about have to do with job markets? Does it have to do with new requirements for getting into college? In other words, are there actual changes in these areas of life to account for new pressures that a previous generation didn't have? When my grandfather was young, he could still find it reasonable to go to work for his whole life in a factory, though his generation had to fight enormous pressures by forming labor unions to get better wages. I don't see young people facing that today.

Or does this pressure young people face today have to do with the breakdown of the nuclear family structure? Does it concern technology?

In examining your lists, try to eliminate those things that overlap. For example, young people in both generations have faced shrinking job markets. But find this out. College tuition has certainly gone up, so we might truly consider that this is a pressure young people didn't face in the 1960s and '70s. Certainly another pressure is the war in Iraq, though this is apparently not a pressure for most young people today as it was for young people in the 1960s, when the military draft loomed as a reality after high school graduation. On the other hand, the generational stereotype for many youth today is that of the slacker. Is this fair? Does it capture today's generation? This might constitute a project in and of itself—both where the stereotype originated and what keeps it going. In what way could young people in the 1960s and '70s also have been cast as slackers? After all, they avoided going to war, and many of them did drugs.

Obviously, your research will require you to challenge your stereotypes. It will require you to conduct some interviews with people, getting them to talk frankly about their pasts, about their perceptions of their lives. Some of these interviews might help you find new sources you did not know about.

The Effects of Poverty

"We all know that money is the root of all kinds of evil, but what about poverty?"

Does poverty cause evil? Begin by looking at the effects of poverty on learning for children, on the lifestyles of single mothers or fathers, on the prospects of communities where incomes are low. Focus on one of these aspects of poverty and work toward proposing a solution to these effects—in one area, education, for example. If possible, conduct interviews with people of different social classes to discover their life experiences as well as their opinions. Out of this material and your secondary research, compose a paper that advocates solutions other than the No Child Left Behind act, which has handcuffed so many teachers and made learning into a game of fact finding described above.

feature 6.5 Writing Prompt Reflection

Consider the ideas presented in this chapter and write an essay in which you refute the ideas here, add to them in meaningful ways, or find both points of agreement and disagreement. Could you see, for example, a writer for television ever needing to conduct research?

Asian Stereotypes in the Media

In February 2012, point guard Jeremy Lin led the New York Knicks to victory with a winning streak in the NBA. Raised in Palo Alto and a graduate from Harvard University, he is one of the few Americans of Chinese decent playing for the NBA, and his humility and skill caught the attention of Americans everywhere. Unfortunately, along with fame came stereotypical publicity which included Lin's picture with a fortune cookie and the line, "The Knicks' Good Fortune," displayed after a winning game (*USA Today*). Insensitive advertisements are just a part of Asian people's typical role on TV, which taints the way most Asians are portrayed. Asians and Asian Americans alike are misrepresented by stereotypes in the media.

Media has a history of blurring the lines of reality. In *Life the Movie*, Neal Gabler discusses how "life itself was gradually becoming a medium all its own, like television, radio, print, and film" (4). This was a problem in twentieth century America because "Americans increasingly lived in a world where fantasy [was] more real than reality" (Gabler 4). In *Technologies of History: Visual Media and the Eccentricity of the Past,* Steve Anderson argues that, "[Movies] may be 'fantastic' (meaning that they may move well into the fictional realm) ... and ... they work to confuse the boundary between fact and fiction" (18). In *How Art Made the World*, Nigel Spivey explains, "our brains are hardwired to concentrate perceptive focus upon objects ... or those parts of objects that matter most" (59). According to Spivey, humans pay attention to what matters most so American entertainment provided America with what the audience wanted to see. Alas, exaggeration and stereotypes, though often "fantastic," provided the audience with easily recognizable characters and familiarity instead of displaying the truth and reality. For the sake of entertainment, "America has developed into a 'carnival culture' or 'trash culture,' where everything is coarsened, vulgarized and trivialized" (Gabler 9). Thus, when Asians are portrayed in the media, there is an automatic stereotype that misrepresents Asians and Asian Americans, and this is dangerous because "the media has a profound effect in making people believe the stereotypes they see" (Tewari, Alvarez 434).

Asians have been portrayed stereotypically in the media since their introduction to Hollywood. Asians in general were also received and perceived negatively in America since the Chinese Exclusion Act in 1882. This was passed to prevent the Chinese from immigrating in to the United States, marking a historical point from which racial misunderstanding by Westerners of Asians would arise (Leon 58). From here, the Chinese and all Asians along with them were perceived by Americans as "others," which set the stage for stereotypes regarding any Asian portrayal. In the article, "Asian American Cinema," Glenn Masuchika claims, "Since the beginning of cinema, Asians have been denied their own faces and voices. 'Orientals' were created out of the fantasies of non-Asians who decided what Asians are 'truly' like without ever allowing Asians to speak for themselves." This was achieved through yellowface, where non-Asians would use yellow theatrical face paint and eye-pulling makeup (Masuchika). From the beginning, Western view of all things related to Asian heritage were generalizations which were reflected in how they were portrayed in the media. In *Hollywood Asian: Philip Ahn and the Politics of Cross-Ethnic Performance*, Hye Seung Chung discusses the "images of 'good' Orientals as a counterpoint to established 'yellow peril' stereotypes, such as... the 'dragon lady'" from the 1930s and 1940s (60). "Good Orientals" included action heroes and romantic heroines while "yellow peril" images included any characters that displayed Western fear of Oriental "vexations and fears of miscegenation" (60). Early actors and actresses of Asian descent found themselves playing stereotypical roles that did not fit their Asian-American identities. In *The China Mystique: Pearl S. Buck, Anna May Wong, Maylin Soong, and the Transformation of American Orientalism*, Karen Leong describes the life and career of Anna May Wong, an early Asian-American actress who made it in Hollywood, and her dilemma in being type-cast. Leong proclaims, "As someone who portrayed the perpetual foreigner in Hollywood films, Wong constantly redefined herself as a Chinese American in relation to shifting international relationships and competing national interests within the film industry" (57). With the rising popularity in martial arts films, martial arts experts also played a significant role in producing Asian stereotypes in Hollywood. Bruce Lee, Jet Li, and Jackie Chan were and are among the many Asian fighters in film and media who portray comedic and epic fighting skills in movies such as, *Drunken Master, The Way of the Dragon*, and *The Shaolin Temple*. From action heroes to evil "yellow peril" characters, Asians and Asian-Americans were introduced by the media as stereotypical characters.

In the media, Asians are stereotypically displayed as one foreign culture group. In *Asian American Women and Men: Labor, Laws, and Love,* Yen Le Espiritu argues, "A central aspect of racial exploitation centers on defining [all Asians] as 'other'" (99). In *Breaking the Bamboo Ceiling: Career Strategies for Asians*, Jane Hyun observes, "Non-Asian Americans often think of Asians as a homogeneous group of people" (1). Examples of this in the media include the movie *Hot Chicks*, where a woman with an obvious Chinese accent plays a Korean mother who cannot pronounce Korean dishes correctly. Her daughter's form of the Korean traditional dress is also incorrectly worn. Also, since the early use of yellowfacing, the exaggeration of Asian slanted eyes has continued to dominate as a stereotypical Asian feature. Though slanted eyes are an Asian facial characteristic, not all Asians have the monolid, but since the introduction of Asian characters in media, the slanted eye has been a stereotype overused and abused. This has led to shows like Family Guy displaying all Asian characters with slits for eyes. In *Asian American Studies: A Reader*, Jean Yu-wen Shen and Min Song disclose how "... Asians as a homogenous group ... implies Asians are 'all alike' and conform to 'types'" (431). Media has a tendency to group all Asian people as simply Asians, without regard to the countries that make up the Asian continent. These countries include Korea, China, Taiwan, Vietnam, Japan, the Philippines, and many more, but the media will not typically acknowledge these differences in culture. Anna May Wong played characters from ethnic backgrounds ranging from Indian to Asian to Eskimo (Leong 64). In the movie *Sixteen Candles*, there is an Asian character named Long Duk Dong, who is supposedly Chinese but is shown wearing Japanese clothes and even speaking Japanese. In media, Asians are typically displayed as Asians without respect to the different aspects and cultures within the group, a stereotype unfair to different Asian cultures. "The term 'Asian-American' is extraordinarily broad, embracing members of many ethnic groups" (*New York Times*).

Entertainment and media have limited Asian women by portraying them as stereotypical characters. "Asian women have been depicted as super feminine, in the image of the 'China Doll,' but also as castrating, in the image of the 'Dragon Lady'" (Espiritu 99). Anna May Wong was a Chinese-American actress in early film and her first few roles were as a character named Lotus Flower and as a Mongol slave girl (Leong 64). She repeated this slave girl role in other characters because they were the ones available to her, and they "[embodied] the exotic and highly sexualized female" (Leong 64). This stereotype was commonly recognized as the Geisha Girl, Lotus Blossom, War Bride, China Doll, or Vietnamese Prostitute (Espiritu 107). These stereotypical portrayals of Asian women have damaged the common perception of regular Asian and Asian American women. Espiritu maintains, "These stereotypes of Asian women as submissive and dainty sex objects not only have impeded women's economic mobility, but also have fostered an enormous demand for X-rated films and pornographic materials" (107). Anna May Wong also played Tiger Lily, a native American, in *Peter Pan* (1924), portraying herself and all women similar to her ethnic background as "primitive, aggressive, and uncivilized" (Leong 64). Asian women were limited to display very specific roles implying a set number of characteristics Asian women could have. Women of Asian descent would play roles where they "often portrayed the tragic Oriental beauty who falls in love with a Euro-American male and either kills herself out of love ... or threatens to kill the Euro-American female who is the object of her love's desire" (Leong 64). This Asian female character represents over-sexualized women who are uncivilized or dependent on a white man and are displayed in shows like *Gunsmoke* and *How the West Was Won* (Espiritu 107). "Cast as sexually available, Asian women become yet another possession of the white man" (Espiritu 107). This is a dangerous stereotype for Asian women because "within a system of racial and gender oppression, the sexual possession of women ... of color by white men becomes yet another means of enforcing unequal power relations" (Espiritu 108).

Asian men have been stereotypically presented by the media. In *Asian American Sexual Politics: The Construction of Race, Gender, and Sexuality,* Rosalind Chou reports, "The assumptions ... for ... Asian American men [are]: they are weak, passive, and effeminate" (168). Asian men are constantly cast as waiters or servers, which demonstrates them as weak or feminine. Espiritu reveals, "By trapping [Asian] men in the stereotypical 'feminine' tasks of serving white men, American society erases the figure of the Asian 'masculine' plantation ... or railroad construction worker ..., thus perpetuating the myth of the androgynous and effeminate Asian man" (104). An example of this in the media is in the movie *Deuce Bigalow: European Gigalow,* where "Asian male sexuality and inferiority function as a joke" (Ono, Pham 72). Another stereotype on the opposite end of the spectrum is the Asian man's hyper masculinity. In *American Masculinities: A Historical Encyclopedia,* Bret Carroll concludes, "The popularity of martial arts films promoted an image of Asian hyper masculinity" (40). This stereotype appeared with characters in the media such as Bruce Lee and Jackie Chan and produced the idea that all Asians knew martial arts, yet the media portrays Asian men as undesirable in different ways. "Asian and Asian American men have often been characterized as a yellow peril, as physical threats, gangsters, or martial arts foes" (Ono, Pham 71). Most attempts to display Asian men in the media have been negative and stereotypical. "The motion picture industry has been key in the construction of Asian men as sexual deviants" (Espiritu 104). This was another aspect of the Yellow Peril, and Asian men were depicted as sexually undesirable. "The movie industry ... castrates Asian males ... [Even when] depicting sexual aggression, this image of a rapist ... casts Asian men as sexually undesirable" (Espiritu 104). Ultimately, Asian men are depicted as inferior as men by the media. "Overall, the dominant culture constructs Asian and Asian American men as desexualized, hence as less powerful than and inferior to all other men" (Ono, Pham 71).

Nowadays, Asians and Asian Americans are portrayed as overly-studious academic achievers; in other words, they are nerds. Ono and Pham illustrate this stereotype by observing, "This representation of ... the geeky computer nerd continues to appear in contemporary media representations" (71). This image of high-achieving Asians in America was portrayed by characters like Data in *The Goonies* and Hiro Nakaruma in *Heroes.* It is still being portrayed in the media in shows like *Glee*, where Asian American students Tina Chang and Mike Chang are constantly shown needing to impress their parents with good grades. *New York Times* reporter Tamar Lewin reveals, "... Stereotypes about Asian Americans ... [include] the perception that they cluster in science, technology, engineering, and math." Asians are all expected to have perfect grades, play an instrument, and be over-achievers by society because of the way they are shown in the media. There are not many characters of Asian descent in American media to begin with, and when there are, the nerd stereotype is commonly displayed. "Asian Americans are traditionally underrepresented in the media and misrepresented with stereotypes, such as the ... nerd stereotype" (*Communication Currents*). These all suggest weakness or lacking in character for Asians in society, and for those who do not know many Asians or Asian-Americans, these misrepresentations are all they have to learn about Asian and Asian-American culture. Robert T. Teranishi, N.Y.U. education professor, explains, "Certainly there's a lot of Asians doing well, at the top of the curve, and that's a point of pride, but there are just as many struggling at the bottom of the curve, and we [want] to draw attention to that" (*New York Times*).

There are some who argue that stereotypes are just a way of organizing people into groups and that this is important for society. In *Stereotype as Explanations: the Formation of Meaningful Beliefs about Social Groups*, Craig McGarthy, Vincent Yzerbyt, and Russell Spears claim, "... unless individuals also perceive themselves to belong to groups, that is, to share characteristics, circumstances, values and beliefs with other people, then society would be without structure or order" (1). According to this opinion, stereotypes exist for people to be grouped together; therefore, they are beneficial to society. However, though stereotypes do exist because there are people of certain groups who typically portray certain characteristics, reinforcing stereotypes damage society because they misrepresent ethnic groups affiliated with the stereotypes. In "What are they like? Non-Expert Definitions of Stereotypes and Their Implications for Stereotypes Maintenance," Anastacia Kurylo defends, "Participants who view stereotypes as accurate, appropriate, and valuable ways to understand target groups may use stereotypes despite the prescription of avoidance and may, thus, maintain stereotypes." The belief that stereotypes are true only provides a cycle of ignorance.

Some believe that stereotyping is beneficial because it saves time and effort. Kendra Campbell, MD in psychiatry/mental health, claims, "After all, stereotypes are actually a good thing. A stereotype is a mental shortcut, which allows us to save time and simplify the quantity of information available to us" (RateMDs). However, stereotypes are generalizations and not always true, and they may provide people like professionals and doctors with false information. Yoonsun Choi, an assistant professor at the United States Social Security

Administration and a faculty associate at the Chapin Hall Center for Children, refutes that stereotypes are good by asserting, "It is critical that researchers look beyond the stereotype so as not to run the risk of perpetuating false perceptions in research and theory" (SSA.UChicago.edu). The truth can be blurred by the use of stereotypes, therefore causing more harm to patients and research subjects, not to mention cultures who are stereotyped in society.

From yellow-facing to portrayals of nerds, sexualized women or effeminate men, and Oriental homogenous groups in the media, Asians and Asian Americans alike have been misrepresented and limited through their stereotypes. Contrary to popular belief due to the media, the Asian continent is consisted of numerous countries and cultures and is filled with many different people. Asian Americans are citizens just like white, black, and Latino Americans, who are also Americans influenced from their ethnic roots. Stereotypes in the media should start acknowledging the average American citizen, regardless of where his or her parents emigrated from, so that society can see beyond stereotypical characters when they look at Asians and Asian Americans.

Works Cited

Alvarez, Alvin and Nita Tewari. *Asian American Psychology: Current Perspectives*. New York: Psychology, 2009. Print.

Anderson, Steve F. *Technologies of History: Visual Media and the Eccentricity of the Past*. Hanover, NH: Dartmouth College, 2011. Print.

Campbell, Kendra. "Should Doctors Stereotype Their Patients?" *RateMDs.com*. N.p., 2 May 2011. Web. 1 Dec. 2012.

Carroll, Bret E. "Asian American Manhood." *American Masculinities: A Historical Encyclopedia. Vol. 1*. Thousand Oaks, CA: Sage Publications, 2003. 38-41. Print.

Chou, Rosalind S. *Asian American Sexual Politics: The Construction of Race, Gender, and Sexuality*. Lanham, MD: Rowman & Littlefield, 2012. Print.

Chung, Hye Seung. *Hollywood Asian: Philip Ahn and the Politics of Cross-ethnic Performance*. Philadelphia: Temple UP, 2006. Print.

Espiritu, Yen Le. *Asian American Women and Men: Labor, Laws and Love*. Thousand Oaks, CA: Sage Publications, 1997. Print.

Gabler, Neal. *Life the Movie: How Entertainment Conquered Reality*. New York: Knopf, 1998. Print.

Hyun, Jane. *Breaking the Bamboo Ceiling: Career Strategies for Asians*. New York: Harper Business, 2005. Print.

Leong, Karen J. *The China Mystique: Pearl S. Buck, Anna May Wong, Mayling Soong, and the Transformation of American Orientalism*. Berkeley, CA: University of California, 2005. Print.

Lewin, Tamar. "Report Takes Aim at 'Model Minority' Stereotype of Asian-American Students." *The New York Times*, 10 June 2008. Web. 12 Nov. 2012.

Masuchika, Glenn. "Asian American Cinema." *Asian American Cinema.* Penn State University Libraries, 24 Sept. 2012. Web. 12 Nov. 2012.

McCarthy, Michael. "Asian Stereotypes Appearing in Coverage of Knicks' Jeremy Lin." *USA Today.* 16 Feb. 2012: n. pag. Web. 11 Nov. 2012.

Ono, Kent A. and Vincent N. Pham. *Asian Americans and the Media.* Cambridge, UK: Polity, 2009. Print.

"Perceptions of Asian American Students: Stereotypes and Effects." *Communication Currents 5.1* (2010): n. pag. A Publication of the National Communication Association. Web. 11   Nov. 2012.

Spivey, Nigel Jonathan.*How Art Made the World.* London: BBC, 2005. Print.

Wu, Jean Yu-wen Shen, and Min Song. *Asian American Studies: A Reader.* New Brunswick, NJ: Rutgers UP, 2000. Print.

rating diversity shouldn't be an acceptable alternative to seeking economic equality.

Grammar Interlude 6: Commas

Commas—Following Introductory Words/Phrases/ Clauses; Comma Splices; Semicolon; Colon

Note: When many of us were in late elementary and early junior high school, our teachers told us to put a comma where we breathed. This unhelpful advice theorizes punctuation as a tool for enunciation. But in modern English punctuation, commas, semicolons, and colons are generally used as structure markers, used to mark off the main clause—where the main subject-verb statement occurs.

1. **Comma following introductory material—usually needed to point to the main clause**.

Main clause: Burt stepped on the DVD player.
SUBJECT: Burt
VERB: stepped (or particle "stepped on")
DIRECT OBJECT: DVD player

If we want to add some statement of cause-effect to this main clause, such as "because he was still very tired," then we will need a comma if we add it at the beginning.

Because he was still very tired, Burt stepped on the DVD player.

(Note the comma after "tired.")

Burt stepped on the DVD player because he was still very tired. (Note that no comma is needed—the subject at the beginning of the main clause is clear.)

Note what sometimes happens when this important comma is omitted:

In the morning sunlight on the floor was warm for the cat to sleep in.
(The reader may have to stop to read this sentence more than once to determine that the subject is "sunlight." But placing a comma after "morning" to mark off the prepositional phrase from the main clause clears up the confusion nicely.)
In the morning, sunlight on the floor was warm for the cat to sleep in.

This rule about a comma following introductory material also applies to words:

However, they thought differently when Ron returned alone.
Yesterday, all my troubles seemed so far away.
Incidentally, my cousin appeared as an extra in that film.
Therefore, Socrates was a mortal.

In each case, the introductory word is marked off from the main clause.

Ex. Choose three passages and put a brick around the main, independent clause. Put a squiggly line under introductory material and, if the writer has failed to, put the comma where it belongs.

Bring these three passages to class for presentation and discussion.

Chapter *Seven*

What We Talk about When
We Talk about Style

Chapter Overview

The argument made in this chapter concerns assumptions many people have about style—that it is only a question of word choice and nothing more. We can change our style, so the argument goes, and not change what we are saying. Furthermore, style is a matter of personal choice, and one style is not better than another.

The evidence of this chapter is that these ideas do not hold up. When we change the style of something, we change content—we are actually saying something different than we were before. And a style is not merely a personal preference, like a favorite color. Rather, there are good, bad, and indifferent styles.

The chapter defines style in terms of sentence length and word choice. Sentence lengths and types are explained, and then tone is discussed. Style appropriateness is given in a discussion of how many people approach writing e-mails.

Matters of Style and Content

Style is sometimes seen as a deeply personal choice, something that cannot be learned but simply "is." According to this view, style is a personal, habitual way of doing something. "That's just my style," some will say, as if no one can criticize this. After all, it's a personal preference, and obviously others have their own styles, which are just as valid and acceptable.

When framed in this way as a personal choice, criticism seems wrong, since it is to say you like one style more than another, and this choice "is entirely subjective." People who say these things will often make similar claims about their opinions. "It's just my opinion," they say, as though this removes it from criticism. "Everyone has an opinion, and this one is mine." But this ignores the very high probability that some opinions are based on good reasons more than others are. It ignores a very rich discussion about what goes into forming opinions and

feature 7.1   Writing Prompt 7

Changing Your Style Is More than a Wardrobe Decision

Consider the following three utterances.

Good morning, Professor Wainwright.

Hey colleague.

Yo, dude.

All three, of course, are recognizable as speech acts particular to one situation, that of giving a greeting. Whatever else we might say in terms of analyzing them, we could argue that while all three are greetings, all three are different. Because of word choice, they convey a different tone. We might even argue that the differences in word choice result in differences in terms of their content. What makes them different, what actually changes their content, is the words that are chosen. They are different in content because they are different in style.

Here is how I would represent the different kinds of content. Each registers a different level of familiarity/formality, and each represents a different relationship between speaker and auditor. The differences between these three utterances might also lead us to speculate on the situation, on who is speaking, and on who is being addressed. The first sounds like someone who is not on familiar terms with a professor. It is shaped around the idea of respect. The second utterance is also a greeting, but it expresses the greeting of an equal. But even this one is different from the last, which implies not only a familiarity but also, depending on the audience for it, an attitude—especially if this speaker is addressing a professor. In that case, we might even appreciate the lack of a desire to "kiss up" to the professor, as this speaker might put it.

For many readers, style means many things, not just sentences and words. It means also genre. It can also mean attitude. Unfortunately, regardless of how they define it, most do not consider style to be a part of one's meaning. For most people who think about it even the slightest bit, style is, like rhetoric, just a wrapper, an external flair brought to substance, not something that changes anything about content. If this is true, then the three utterances given above are all one and the same. Anyone listening to the words, however, and how they register something concrete about the human situation and relationships that they evoke, will conclude that these are very different in terms of their content.

feature 7.2 Swirling colors

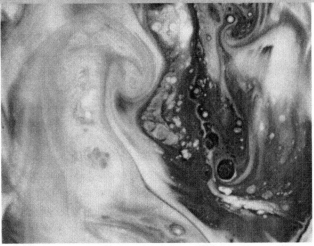

© Karin Lamprecht, 2009. Used under license of Shutterstock, Inc.

the need to support them. It suggests that any opinion, even one founded mainly on prejudice and lack of experience, is as good as opinions arrived at after much thought and study.

The same can be said of style. The person who says "those fragments and ellipses and incidents of verbal repetition are just my style" might be invoking a real stylist she has read, and we should not ignore the fact that there are good and even better ways to say something.

Consider the following two passages. Consider the theme or subject and also how the style elaborates or develops the theme:

Okay, a new book. This author is cool. This author rocks. This author is my favorite. This author knows how to write. Telling a story. That's what it's about. The only thing.

In his new novel, Stephen King tells a vivid, shocking story. For those who come back to him book after book, they are looking for a good story. And this author knows how to deliver.

Does the meaning stay the same in these two passages? Does the first one, so different in sentence structure and word choice from the second, say the same thing that the second one does? Is one clearer, more readable than the other? The first, certainly, relies on quick phrases, even sentence fragments. But it does not say quite the same thing that the second passage does. In the second passage, where the sentences are complete, longer than the first, though not much longer, the writer seems to direct the reader to certain conclusions that are not made in the first. What the first passage also says, however, is something about the writer of the passage. More than just style is at work here. We might very well conclude that the writer of the second passage is more reliable and thoughtful than the writer of the first. In these two instances, we can see that style changes meaning, but it also influences *ethos*.

This is all to say that style is important and part of meaning. Certainly some writers are noted for their style, but these writers acknowledge that style was not something they simply had. Rather, the style they discovered came after much focus on their subject. Only as they continued to write and revise their work, sometimes over two decades, did their distinctive style emerge. This is very different from the person who never writes except for class, and who says, "this is just my style, and you can't criticize it." We certainly can criticize it, and the writer may learn from such criticism. After all, it is clear that some styles are based on more work, reason, and analysis than others. In fact, we might consider here that "that's just my style" or "my opinion" might be considered the last hold out of the uninformed who wants to remain so, the ultimate claim of the person who wants to stop all discussion.

feature 7.3 Abstract background

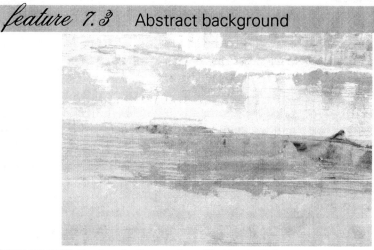

© S-BELOV, 2009. Used under license from Shutterstock, Inc.

A Brief Definition: Clarity about Style

While style is a word that is vaguely and inconsistently applied to any number of ideas, in the following discussion we will think about style in terms of the following:

- Patterns of sentences chosen by a writer: compound, complex, simple
- Various lengths of sentences chosen by a writer
- Word choice, as well as levels of diction
- The presence or absence of metaphor and other forms of figurative language
- How tone, as for example, in irony, can be established.

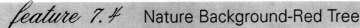

feature 7.4   Nature Background-Red Tree

© selanik, 2009. Used under license from Shutterstock, Inc.

These different aspects of language use will constitute our study in this chapter. They lead us to thinking not only about how style is achieved, but also what different styles mean.

Writing Composition

Examine features 7.3 and 7.4 for subjects and style. First, what is the subject of each. Establish this. Then explain similarities and differences in style. How does style influence or change the subject in each? How does it change meaning? Be prepared to defend your answers.

Style: Beginnings in Grammatical Sentence Patterns

Instead of claiming that what we do naturally is therefore good, I suggest a beginning to style in the first item listed above: Sentence patterns. The ideal style is, vaguely, that which is most suited for the occasion and the hearers. In front of second graders, most teachers keep their sentences short and directive, their words simple. In front of college students, the continuous short sentences and simple language will strain hearers, sound insulting, and suggest arrested writing development on the part of the writer. It should be added that reading levels for books are determined mainly by sentence complexity, length, and word choice. This is much more helpful than saying something about appropriateness. To be more helpful, it should be said that the best style is appropriate in terms of sentence lengths and word choice, and the best, most interesting style is that which uses more than one sentence type.

In standard written English, there are four basic sentence patterns that writers mix, match, exploit, and play with. Sometimes writers combine these four into greater sums. And they often add phrases to mix things up. The four sentence patterns are **simple**, **compound**, **complex**, and **compound- complex**. Some add the effective **sentence fragment**, as opposed to the weak fragment written unwittingly, to form a fifth pattern. Some beginning writers talk of their style as though they would throw out all rules and regulations and just be creative, but there really are four (or five) patterns they will choose from over and over.

Simple Sentences

A simple sentence consists of one subject-verb unit that is a complete thought.

John slept.

In this sentence, "John" is the noun, and "slept" is the verb.

This is a simple sentence.

Here are more simple sentences which, I hope, demonstrate the simple sentence's variety. In each, identify the subject, verb, and whatever else is going on in the sentence, the direct object, the subject complement.

I am going home.
Jake ate the candy bar.
I love Greek food.
Cindy has a gambling problem.
Ralph fed the ducks.
John slept in the park.
We're all over eighteen here.
In the morning, Bert kissed his wife and gave her flowers.

How is the last one simple? It has two verbs. And this is true: It has "kissed" and "gave" as the two verbs in the sentence. However, there is still only one subject doing the kissing and giving. This is still a simple sentence, but this time there is a variation on the others before it. It is a simple sentence with a compound verb, "kissed" and "gave."

We might also be thrown off by the beginning of that last sentence, with "In the morning." Doesn't that make it something other than simple? No. "In the morning" is a prepositional phrase, this time serving as an adverbial phrase that simply modifies when Bert kissed and gave. A phrase does not make a simple sentence complex. A phrase will have only a noun or a verb, not a noun and a verb. For example, we could take the first sentence above, "John slept," and add a phrase to either end of it:

In the morning, John slept.
Or
John slept in the morning.

Notice that a comma is needed in the first sentence because the phrase appears at the beginning of the sentence as an introduction. In the second example, it does not. Nevertheless, in both cases, we would still have a simple sentence that also has a prepositional phrase. Here are some other phrases:

at the race track
on the heals of their first victory (this actually has two phrases)
at the palace the other night (this one also has two phrases)
without his wife
into the stormy seas
without relief

Take note. Not one of these will have what it takes to change a simple sentence into a complex one. This means that a simple sentence can take on modifiers, even second verbs, getting pretty long, and yet still be simple.

In the morning, wearing his slippers, before breakfast, in the kitchen, Bert lovingly kissed his beautiful, tan, twenty-five year old wife with bleached blonde hair and gave her red and pink roses.

This is a simple sentence. It is long—it is made long by modifying phrases (in the morning, wearing his slippers, with bleached blonde hair, etc.), adverbs (lovingly), and adjectives (beautiful, tan, twenty-five-year-old, blonde, red, pink). It may be overwritten, but it is still a simple sentence. It has one subject (Bert) and verb unit (kissed and gave).

Obviously, a passage composed of only simple sentences, unless some of them are heavily modified and lengthened, will sound stilted, choppy, and even meaningless. For example, take the following passage:

I think she's a hypocrite. A hypocrite says one thing but does the opposite. Someone like this is not true. They are people who try to get away with things. The things hypocrites try to get away with are looking good in public. But they are as bad as everybody else. They aren't better than everybody, they're worse.

There are other problems with this passage, but to begin, except for the sixth sentence, this is composed of all simple, short sentences, making it sound monotonous, like the speaker who drones. To avoid this, use other patterns in the English sentence repertoire.

Compound Sentences

A compound sentence has two simple sentences joined by a comma and a coordinating conjunction or by a semicolon. (The main use of the semicolon in modern English is to join two simple sentences, also known as independent clauses.)

Here are the coordinating conjunctions:

For
And
Nor
But
Or
Yet
So

Notice that you can remember the coordinating conjuctions and differentiate them from subordinating conjunctions and words like "however" and "therefore" by the acrostic FANBOYS. Each coordinating conjunction suggests equal, not subordinate, ideas, and provides a logical joining of them. For example,

John slept in the morning, but I couldn't.

In this case, the simple sentence "John slept" is joined to the simple sentence "I couldn't." This is a compound sentence. The following will give us more examples of the pattern:

I went to the show, but I didn't see her there.
I've decided to vote for the Democrat this year, and Sally is voting
    Republican.
Jonathon ate the same fish we did, yet he didn't become sick.
In the morning, in his slippers, in the kitchen, Bert gave his beautiful,
    twenty-five-year-old, bleach blonde wife the red and pink roses,
    and she happily kissed him.

Obviously, to vary sentence patterns and lengths, sparingly add modifying words and phrases, and switch from simple to compound sentences. Or, better, add a third device, the complex sentence.

Complex Sentences

A third pattern, the complex sentence, consists of a simple sentence and a dependent clause. For example,

When he was twenty-six, Nazar played in a rock band.

The first part of this sentence, "When he was twenty-six," is a dependent clause. Look closely at it. A clause has a subject and a verb; in this case the pronoun "he" is the subject and "was" is the verb. This makes it different from a phrase, such as "in the morning." This is what makes the two following sentences different; one begins with a phrase, and is a simple sentence, and the second begins with a dependant clause and is a complex sentence:

In the morning, John slept. (simple sentence)

When he took his vacation, John slept in the morning. (complex sentence)

Another name for the dependent clause, if it is punctuated with a period as though it were a sentence, is "fragment." It certainly has a subject and a verb, two features of the complete sentence. But the subordinate conjunction or relative pronoun at the start makes it dependent and an unfinished thought. We can usually hear this difference, as with the following:

When he took his vacation

Most of us would for more information. When he took his vacation, what happened? We would want more explanation. The following in bold print are dependent clauses. Each one of them turns a simple sentence into a complex sentence.

After we returned from the museum, I made us dinner.
Sally, **who was just trying to break even,** moved to the slot machines.
The metal rod **that finally broke and caused the collapse** was too old
    to withstand the strong winds.
When I finish school, I'm going to Europe for six months.

In each case, a subject-verb unit is also subordinated, or made dependent, to a main idea expressed in the simple sentence it is attached to. Note that "who" and "that" are relative pronouns that serve, like pronouns, as stand ins for the main subject or noun so that we don't have to sound repetitious.

Compound-Complex Sentences

The fourth sentence type is the compound-complex, or complex-compound sentence. This is a sentence that combines one or more dependent clauses (when Bert was an athlete, before I became pregnant with my fifth child, if I decide to study piano) with a compound sentence. The following are examples. In each, identify the dependent clause and the compound sentence:

1. Before I became pregnant with my fifth child, I was happily married, and my husband was making enough money to support us.
2. When I was a child, I spoke as a child; I thought as a child.
3. The wizard, who stood six feet tall, could make himself disappear, yet he wasn't moving from the dangerous room.
4. Though there were many casualties, the crew leader decided to stay the course, and no one could change his mind.

These are the four sentence patterns of English: simple, compound, complex, and compound-complex sentences. Writers use them to create variety and rhythm in their prose. They also add phrases and modifying words.

Practice

1. Just for the practice, use the four patterns, simple, compound, complex, and compound-complex to explain, in your own words, what these four patterns are.
2. When you have finished 1, look at a paragraph of your own writing. Rewrite it using various sentence patterns described here. See if it isn't better.

Doing a Remix

In focusing on the first four sentence types, we can talk about style that is effective and style that is not. In academic writing, the sentence fragment is not effecive. What is valued is writing that follows standard rules for grammar and has sentences that are varied in length and pattern. Writing that has unplanned repetition and short sentences is not valued. Again, take the following paragraph about hypocrites as an example:

I think she's a hypocrite. A hypocrite is someone who says one thing but does the opposite. Someone who says one thing and does the opposite is not true. They are people who try to get away with things. The things hypocrites try to get away with are looking good in public. But they are as bad as everybody else. They aren't better than everybody, they're worse.

As we noted above, this is a passage in which sentences are all short (the longest is eleven words long) and all simple. The last sentence, the one that tries to be compound rather than simple like the others before it, is missing the "and" after the comma and is a comma splice, which doesn't break the rhythm established by the simple, short sentences before it. Notice also that all of the five sentences are not only simple but constructed around the passive verb "to be," and offer only the simple "A is B" or "A = B" equation, as in "someone who says one thing and does the opposite is not true."

In contrast, the desired style is one in which the writer varies these sentence patterns. Consider the following passage, which might be written for young readers:

The wizard could make himself disappear. He was six feet tall. The warthog came in. It was seven feet tall. The wizard wasn't moving from the dangerous room. The wizard took out his wand. The wizard waved his wand. The warthog laughed. The warthog disappeared.

This choppy passage is afflicted with a style that is composed of nothing but simple sentences. Contrast it with the following:

The wizard, who was six feet tall, could make himself disappear, but when the seven-foot-tall warthog came into the room, the wizard didn't move. Instead, he took out his wand, waved it, and the warthog, laughing, disappeared.

This is a better passage in terms of sentence lengths than the previous. It has varied sentences, and this makes for smoother reading and more emphatic meaning. It demonstrates one feature of an effective style, sentences of varied lengths and patterns.

Tone, Irony, and Variation: Style Comparisons

Other distinctive qualities in a good style are tone and voice. These usually have to do with the slant or attitude that the writer has taken to her subject, which can be most prominently reflected through word choice. Clearly, concrete nouns are preferred to vague terms like "things" or "items." Writers generally control their tone by avoiding too many colloquial phrases that we hear in conversations, phrases like "that was a real come down" instead of "he was humiliated," or "back in the day" rather than "once" or "twenty years ago." Granted, these everyday clichés of conversation are often used in opinion essays in the daily paper, and they can be used to enliven a speech, but in certain genres they are not appropriate. As with everything suggested in this section, it is important to consider audience and genre when deciding that a certain phrase or word choice is appropriate. This includes the use of the first and second person pronouns.

Authority in writing is also constructed through a skillful incorporation of source material—especially through the smooth transitions created through signal phrases, the correct use of quotation marks, and punctuation. Along with authority, tone can certainly be affected when we shift in our writing from third person to first person. The presence of the "I" can create a personal dimension, and even this can be further changed when switching to the second person "you," which is used in instructional genres. The switch to the "you" can sometimes change the tone of a piece.

Consider the hypocrite passage above, which begins with the construction "I think. This construction raises the possibility that the only basis for the accusation of hypocrisy is that the writer thinks it is so. There is also other evidence that the passage reads like an accusation, which deepens with the last three sentences repeating the preacherly "they" in reference to hypocrites, not the more inclusive "we." This very simple choice of pronouns—the accusing, finger pointing "you" or "they" makes for a different tone than one in which the writer admits to suffering from the same problems she is describing. Furthermore, the use of these constructions can also convey a tone of informality, which may be less of a problem with certain genres than the preachy and accusatory tone. In the passage above "they" is mindlessly repeated in the last four sentences, as is the deadly ambiguity in "things" and the wooden, basic "someone who says one thing and does the opposite," repeated to connect the first sentence to the second. In contrast to Dickens's planned use of "Monseigneur" to start his sentences below, the repetition about hypocrites comes off as wooden. It sounds as though the writer is not listening to the last passage she wrote. It casts a poor light on the writer. In contrast, consider the following:

Monseigneur had one truly noble idea of general public business, which was, to let everything go on in its own way; of particular public business, Monseigneur had the other truly noble idea that it must all go his way—tend to his own power and pocket. Of his pleasures, general and particular, Monseigneur had the other truly noble idea that the world was made for them. The text of his order (altered from the original by only a pronoun, which is not much) ran: "The earth and the fullness thereof are mine, saith Monseigneur." (Dickens 110)

Notice that "noble" is repeated three times, but it is used for an increasingly ironic tone. We might suggest that the topic of Dickens's paragraph about Monseigneur in *A Tale of Two Cities* is his arrogance. But the way that Dickens develops this quality is so different from the passage above, which comes off as a basic accusation. Instead of six simple sentences, we read three sentences. The first is compound-complex. The second is simple, but it is still longer than any of simple sentences in the first passage. The third is complex. The hypocrisy of this "holy" man is developed through irony, then, with the Monseigneur shown putting his own pleasures that he believes the world was made for before the general public business and welfare, and finally substituting "saith Monseigneur" for "saith the Lord" at the end. Furthermore, in the development of this idea, the phrase "truly noble idea" comes to take on a false ring.

In the final analysis, it is true that both passages presume to treat of hypocrisy. To say that they are both saying basically the same thing is actually wrong, most clearly in the attitude or tone that is established in each. The first passage is a fairly blatant accusation. And while it states that the girl is guilty, in contrast, Dickens's passage shows his character in perhaps the most deadly and spiritually condemning form of hypocrisy, but he does it with a dash of humor. In the final analysis, these two passages are not saying the same thing. For the first, talk of hypocrisy is unclear. For Dickens, hypocrisy has deep spiritual and political effects that are registered in the impoverishment of the general public welfare. While both writers presume to talk of hypocrisy, they say very different things about the topic. Part of this difference is in a stylistic approach, from sentence length (Dickens's sentences build into a tone or feeling), to word choice, to the larger tone of irony rather than blatant accusation.

feature 7.5   Grotesque

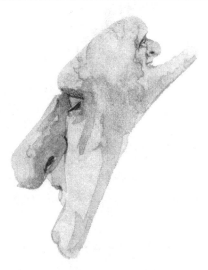

Levels of Style

Style is often separated into different levels based on what is sometimes called "social register," a term that refers generally to the language that is deemed appropriate for different levels of social situations. Four levels of style are observed in this regard: high, middle, conversational (middle and conversational are sometimes seen as the same), and low. Dickens's style, at least in the passage above, might be read today as an example of high style, though in his time Dickens was heard and loved by members of the lower classes. The high style is that which might be reserved for high affairs of state and ceremony. It traditionally has been considered formal, with long sentences and word choice that is elevated and "not common" or "everyday," a style in which we might say "ten-dollar" words suffice. Yet in hearing the Dickens passage, it is possible to understand how it would have been less than formal and even fall on the ears of those unread audiences who flocked to hear him read. Dickens does not use words above the common lot, and only his use of the semicolon and of words from the *King James Bible* like "saith" suggest qualities of high style, at least to our ears today, though he employs them to ironic ends.

The elevated, or high style, is itself hardly a stable category. It might be defined in the way that most styles are, in terms of sentence lengths and word choice. Still, we might see it changing as levels of literacy do. Included in our discussion of literacy might be the texts a culture values as seminal. It would seem that in current debate, the Constitution remains one of these documents, a cultural influence. But it is also a document that some see as open to interpretation and, instead of forming a unified backdrop, takes up the foreground in arguments, for example, over whether the right to privacy is constitutional. In some ways, the high or grand style suggests a series of ideas that present the speaker and hearers with a historical connection and context not available today. This has to do with the thought life of communities. It would appear that certain old documents, or "old rhetorics," as Richard Weaver calls them, provide a constructed historical context, even evoking and naming that context. This can be seen, certainly, in a document like the American Declaration of Independence, which begins with the following historical context (in a fairly developed sentence, too, by the way):

When in the course of human events it becomes necessary for one people to dissolve the political bands which have connected them with another and to assume among the powers of the earth, the separate and equal station to which the Laws of Nature and Nature's god have entitle them, a decent respect to the opinions of mankind requires that they should declare the causes that impel them to the separation.

Few listeners today look to orators for a sense of historical distance or their place in the march of progress and history. We seem private, personal, disconnected, and, many might add, contentedly so. But at the beginning of the American revolt against King George of England, such a context was indeed cited.

Or consider what some think of as Abraham Lincoln's greatest speech, the Gettysburg Address: "Four score and seven years ago, our forefathers brought forth on this continent a new nation, founded on the principles that. . ." Once again, historical distance and context are a given. Style, in this case at least, is not simply word choice or the use of fragments, though even this choice suggests a philosophical perspective. Style also suggests something about the world in which we live. Today, we might not want to write in the style the signers of the Declaration used.

Levels of Style II: E-mail

All of these ideas come from reflection on high or elevated style, especially as it leads us to consider what it might suggest about context, audience, and values. There is value in looking at styles that are no longer in vogue, no longer share a contemporary context, for their strangeness can cause us to reflect on the thinking behind them. In contrast to the grand style, of course, informal or conversational style requires a written style that is closer to everyday speech, and allows for shorter sentences and words that are common and accessible. And then there is the low style. If we were to consider, for example, the typical style of the e-mail between friends in the terms we've used above, what would it suggest about the cultural context of the moment?

Attempts to define and explain the e-mail have been tricky. When contrasted with other well-known forms, it doesn't quite fit. Some people, certainly, use the e-mail as a convenient way to send letters. And indeed the e-mail sent by an employee from one company to another certainly does retain most of the conventions of the business letter, including the use of standard written English. This requirement has confused some regular users of e-mail, however, who also use it and text messaging as a kind of telegraphic medium for familiar communiqués between close friends. One manager, speaking of conditions in 2000 and 2001, noted that his company, which handled medical technology and million-dollar accounts with clients on a weekly basis, relied heavily on business e-mail. One unfortunate consequence of this arrangement was that his employees were regularly getting the company into trouble by sending e-mails that did not meet the business letter standards, and he reported having to confront employees regularly on improving their communications and actually firing several people every year for sending the kinds of e-mails they'd regularly send to their friends. While these e-mails, with graphics, shorthand, poor spelling and grammar, as well as items like "lol," are certainly appropriate with friends, they reflected badly on this company's image and had no place in business communication. Use of a familiar medium, e-mail, was causing confusion over genre and style. Of particular concern to the manager of these accounts was that his warnings,

feature 7.6   E-mail

© juliegrondin, 2009. Used under license from Shutterstock, Inc.

training, and confrontations with his employees did not bring about change. Many were simply unable to write in any other style than they were used to writing in, and their spelling tended toward the popular, with "rite" instead of "right," "be4" instead of "before," and so forth.

As this manger demonstrates, businesses usually care more about good grammar than English teachers do. In fact, as one educator puts it, the second most important quality business managers look for in those they are hiring is writing ability. Whether this manager's experience with his employee's poor business grammar is a widespread concern, and whether or not his assessment of it was correct, clearly e-mail is a vexed, complicated medium in which genres cannot be clearly defined. Even so, the practices of e-mail users might be shown to reflect a certain viewpoint, when considered as communication. Some analysis can tell us about the rhetoric of this medium.

First, the opening salutation is revealing. When I open my e-mail account, I will regularly find messages coming in from different levels. There will be the business letter from a textbook company which has the date and some form of company identification at the top, and this will be followed by the salutation "Dear Professor," which seems to personalize it, even though this same correspondence has surely been mass mailed to a thousand other teachers. This form seems to replicate in electronic mail the old mass mailed form letter.

Then there will be e-mails similar to this one, except that the e-mail itself is not a letter but an advertisement. No attempt is made to disguise this fact, and no salutation is given. The only evidence that this is addressed to me is my name in the "To" slot. The ad is usually mostly a graphic, with little text.

Both of these kinds of e-mails come as the work of people largely used to using standard English. So are the e-mails from various levels of the administration, from president and provost, to dean and department chair, though our chair seems to have the permission of sending both formal letters ("Dear Colleagues") and quick, witty exchanges over issues that are not open to the whole department. I feel this same difference, writing with less familiarity and greater formality the further up the administrative order I go. In this, e-mail seems to vary between the professional and the private or personal, and it is up to me to understand the different social registers involved. This ability to determine appropriateness of e-mail content and style seems to be based on my own training in writing and rhetoric, and it leads me to consider another type of e-mail I receive from students or from writers whose main medium for correspondence seems to be e-mail.

These e-mails will show a range of interesting features. Some students will write without embarrassment in unreadable syntax with punctuation and spelling errors. Even so, some of these same e-mails will show technological expertise, with attachments and links to Internet sites. I sense that if I were to call them on their rough style, as a business manager would, they would wonder what the "big deal" is. Some students have actually expressed this attitude in discussions about e-mail grammar. The importance, for them, seems to be the "content" of the message, not the wrapping, what I call their *ethos*. (See the discussion at the beginning of this chapter.)

One conclusion we might draw about the rhetoric of the e-mail is that if we are addressing someone more familiarly, we can forget formality and the need in all other kinds of writing for context. We can "be ourselves," which seems to be the great cultural "unity" of a post-PC, post-Internet society in America. But this same "unity" needs to be remembered when using e-mail with strangers or those in positions of authority. Though a value in late democracy is to ignore authority, and e-mail would seem to be the chief communiqué of this new democracy,"

feature 7.7   Internet

© digitalife, 2009. Used under license from Shutterstock, Inc.

this unity doesn't work in every case. Certain readers will always consider badly constructed emails as "poor communication." The more we become public in our e-mails, the more we need to know what is appropriate in word choice and in sentence lengths. E-mail has made the need for a good business style more urgent.

What we have with computer and Internet technology is not less need for good writing, but more of it. Instead of replacing writing, new writing technologies have improved the task of writing and also changed some of the issues for writers. For example, we can send messages instantly, and this has in some ways conveyed the idea that our communications are trivial and light. Writers also have wonderful word processing and publishing programs that allow them to revise text more speedily (for cut-and-paste examples function in the editing menu) and to publish professional documents for pennies. These same technologies have also increased confusion, even as they have led to more writing, not less.

Defining a Good Style

A good or bad style can be defined in terms of appropriateness or inappropriateness for a given occasion. One would probably resist saying "Yo dude" to a supervisor, unless otherwise alerted that he or she prefers this form of address. Similarly, most college writing teachers stress that sentence fragments are not appropriate for academic, college-level writing and will mark these as errors. But so is the formal, elevated style sometimes seen as inappropriate and even affected, as if it is putting on airs, drawing unnecessary attention to one's ethos rather than, as is usually desired, one's subject. In addition to talking about high, middle, and low styles, we often refer to style that is "clear," "muddy," or "concise," and style that is wordy.

But even as we strive to be clear in writing and avoid "verbiage," we should also stress that a style is never transparent, or invisible. Words, in a sense, are always in the way. Words are always carriers of our values, and the words we choose, in this sense, are never neutral or value free.

How to Develop an Appropriate and Effective Style

There is debate about the importance of focusing on style in a writing class, just as there is debate about how to develop a good one. In either case, there is agreement that practice is important, but that any practice, if it is to make anyone "perfect," should be the practice of good habits, not lazy. The habit of careful editing and thinking can support each other.

One suggestion, taken from James Britton and other expressivists like Donald Murray, is to write in expressive forms, especially journaling. Murray advocates also the practice of free writing. Certainly, the continuous practice of journaling can help to develop confidence and fluency in writing. Sometimes the practice of free writing can lead to far more interesting sentences and whole passages than calculated, editing "as we go" writing, where the main concern is with correctness or saying it well. Indeed, the previous passage about a girl who is a hypocrite could stand in for dozens of passages by writers who are worried about committing grammatical errors and saying things "correctly."

There is a paradox in this. Instead of pursuing a certain style, pursue getting an idea down in clear terms. This is how most published stylists have worked. Most published writers do not claim to have gone after a good style. They have claimed to want to develop their ideas the best they can. And through repeated writing, their ideas and a style emerged.

A second suggestion, from practices known from Classical Rhetoric, is imitation. In this practice, select a passage of any length, from a few sentences to a paragraph or a page, and then write an imitation of its sentence patterns but using your own subject.

feature 7.8 Writing Prompt Reflection

In reflecting on the ideas presented in Chapter 7, compose a response to Writing Prompt 7. What points seem most important or most wrong? Develop your perspective on style, considering the ideas presented here.

1. Send a series of e-mails to people, but write them using different levels of style. Begin by writing to your friend about something that happened to you—something good or bad. Then, write about the same issue, but address it to your mom or dad or aunt, and be careful to write it in a series of mixed sentence patterns discussed in this chapter. Write using simple, compound, complex, and compound-complex sentences. Do this by getting your thoughts down first. Then re-read this e-mail, and change the sentences so that they are different from each other. 2) Print up and bring to class several of your e-mails. Analyze them for features of context and style discussed here. How much context is given in it, and to whom is it addressed (very few people I know today care about the proper use of who and whom, and this comes up in their e-mails).

Jonathan Swift

A Modest Proposal

For preventing the children of poor people in ireland from being a burden to their parents or country, and for making them beneficial to the public

It is a melancholy object to those who walk through this great town or travel in the country, when they see the streets, the roads, and cabin doors, crowded with beggars of the female-sex, followed by three, four, or six children, all in rags and importuning every passenger for an alms. These mothers, instead of being able to work for their honest livelihood, are forced to employ all their time in strolling to beg sustenance for their helpless infants, who, as they grow up, either turn thieves for want of work, or leave their dear native country to fight for the Pretender in Spain, or sell themselves to the Barbadoes.

I think it is agreed by all parties that this prodigious number of children in the arms, or on the backs, or at the heels of their mothers, and frequently of their fathers, is in the present deplorable state of the kingdom a very great additional grievance; and therefore whoever could find out a fair, cheap, and easy method of making these children sound, useful members of the commonwealth would deserve so well of the public as to have his statue set up for a preserver of the nation.

But my intention is very far from being confined to provide only for the children of professed beggars; it is of a much greater extent, and shall take in the whole number of infants at a certain age who are born of parents in effect as little able to support them as those who demand our charity in the streets.

As to my own part, having turned my thoughts for many years upon this important subject, and maturely weighed the several schemes of other projectors, I have always found them grossly mistaken in their computation. It is true, a child just dropped from its dam may be supported by her milk for a solar year, with little other nourishment; at most not above the value of two shillings, which the mother may certainly get, or the value in scraps, by her lawful occupation of begging; and it is exactly at one year old that I propose to provide for them in such a manner as instead of being a charge upon their parents or the parish, or wanting food and raiment for the rest of their lives, they shall on the contrary contribute to the feeding, and partly to the clothing, of many thousands.

Jonathan Swift, "A Modest Proposal," 1729.

There is likewise another great advantage in my scheme, that it will prevent those voluntary abortions, and that horrid practice of women murdering their bastard children, alas, too frequent among us, sacrificing the poor innocent babes, I doubt, more to avoid the expense than the shame, which would move tears and pity in the most savage and inhuman breast.

The number of souls in this kingdom being usually reckoned one million and a half, of these I calculate there may be about two hundred thousand couple whose wives are breeders; from which number I subtract thirty thousand couples who are able to maintain their own children, although I apprehend there cannot be so many under the present distresses of the kingdom; but this being granted, there will remain an hundred and seventy thousand breeders. I again subtract fifty thousand for those women who miscarry, or whose children die by accident or disease within the year. There only remain an hundred and twenty thousand children of poor parents annually born. The question therefore is, how this number shall be reared and provided for, which, as I have already said, under the present situation of affairs, is utterly impossible by all the methods hitherto proposed. For we can neither employ them in handicraft or agriculture; we neither build houses (I mean in the country) nor cultivate land. They can very seldom pick up a livelihood by stealing till they arrive at six years old, except where they are of towardly parts; although I confess they learn the rudiments much earlier, during which time they can however be looked upon only as probationers, as I have been informed by a principal gentlemen in the county of Cavan, who protested to me that he never knew above one or two instances under the age of six, even in a part of the kingdom so renowned for the quickest proficiency in that art.

I am assured by our merchants that a boy or girl before twelve years old is no salable commodity; and even when they come to this age they will not yield above three pounds, or three pounds and half a crown at most on the Exchange; which cannot turn to account either to the parents or the kingdom, the charge of nutriment and rags having been at least four times that value.

I shall now therefore humbly propose my own thoughts, which I hope will not be liable to the least objection.

I have been assured by a very knowing American of my acquaintance in London, that a young healthy child well nursed is at a year old a most delicious, nourishing, and wholesome food, whether stewed, roasted, baked or boiled; and I make no doubt that it will equally serve in a fricassee or a ragout.

I do therefore humbly offer it to public consideration that of the hundred and twenty thousand children, already computed, twenty thousand may be reserved for breed, whereof only one fourth part to be males, which is more than we allow to sheep, black cattle, or swine; and my reason is that these children are seldom the fruits of marriage, a circumstance not much regarded by our savages, therefore one male will be sufficient to serve four females. That the remaining hundred thousand may at a year old be offered in sale to the persons of quality and fortune through the kingdom, always advising the mother to let them suck plentifully in the last month, so as to render them plump and fat for a good table. A child will make two dishes at an entertainment for friends; and when the family dines alone, the fore or hind quarter will make a reasonable dish, and seasoned with a little pepper or salt will be very good boiled on the fourth day, especially in winter.

I have reckoned upon a medium that a child just born will weigh twelve pounds, and in a solar year if tolerably nursed increaseth to twenty-eight pounds.

I grant this food will be somewhat dear, and therefore very proper for land-lords, who, as they have already devoured most of the parents, seem to have the best title to the children.

Infant's flesh will be in season throughout the year, but more plentiful in March, and a little before and after. For we are told by a grave author, an emi-nent French physician, that fish being a prolific diet, there are more children born in Roman Catholic countries about nine months after Lent than at any other season: therefore, reckoning a year after Lent, the markets will be more glutted than usual, because the number of popish infants is at least three to one in this kingdom; and therefore it will have one other collateral advantage, by lessening the number of Papists among us.

I have already computed the charge of nursing a beggar's child (in which list I reckon all cottagers, laborers, and four fifths of the farmers) to be about two shillings per annum, rags included: and I believe no gentleman would repine to give ten shillings for the carcass of a good fat child, which, as I have said, will make four dishes of excellent nutritive meat, when he hath only some particular friend or his own family to dine with him. Thus the squire will learn to be a good landlord, and grow popular among the tenants; the mother will have eight shil-lings net profit, and be fit for work till she produces another child.

Those who are more thrifty (as I must confess the times require) may flay the carcass; the skin of which artificially dressed will make admirable gloves for ladies, and summer boots for fine gentlemen.

As to our city of Dublin, shambles may be appointed for this purpose in the most convenient parts of it, and butchers we may be assured will not be want-ing; although I rather recommend buying the children alive, and dressing them hot from the knife as we do roasting pigs.

A very worthy person, a true lover of his country, and whose virtues I highly esteem, was lately pleased in discoursing on this matter to offer a refinement upon my scheme. He said that many gentlemen of this kingdom, having of late destroyed their deer, he conceived that the want of venison might be well sup-plied by the bodies of young lads and maidens, not exceeding fourteen years of age nor under twelve, so great a number of both sexes in every county being now ready to starve for want of work and service; and these to be disposed of by their parents, if alive, or otherwise by their nearest relations. But with due deference to so excellent a friend and so deserving a patriot, I cannot be altogether in his sentiments; for as to the males, my American acquaintance assured me from frequent experience that their flesh was generally tough and lean, like that of our schoolboys, by continual exercise, and their taste disagreeable; and to fatten them would not answer the charge. Then as to the females, it would, I think with humble submission, be a loss to the public, because they soon would become breeders themselves: and besides, it is not improbable that some scrupulous people might be apt to censure such a practice (although indeed very unjustly) as a little bordering upon cruelty; which, I confess, hath always been with me the strongest objection against any project, how well soever intended.

But in order to justify my friend, he confessed that this expedient was put into his head by the famous Psalmanazar, a native of the island Formosa, who came from thence to London above twenty years ago, and in conversation told my friend that in his country when any young person happened to be put to death, the executioner sold the carcass to persons of quality as a prime dainty; and that in his time the body of a plump girl of fifteen, who was crucified for an attempt to poison the emperor, was sold to his Imperial Majesty's prime minister of state, and other great mandarins of the court, in joints from the gibbet, at four hundred crowns, Neither indeed can I deny that if the same use were made of several plump young girls in this town, who without one single groat to their fortunes cannot stir abroad without a chair, and appear at the playhouse and assemblies in foreign fineries which they never will pay for, the kingdom would not be the worse.

Some persons of a desponding spirit are in great concern about that vast number of poor people who are aged, diseased, or maimed, and I have been desired to employ my thoughts what course may be taken to ease the nation of so grievous an encumbrance. But I am not in the least pain upon that matter, because it is very well known that they are every day dying and rotting by cold and famine, and filth and vermin, as fast as can be reasonably expected. And as to the younger laborers, they are now in almost as hopeful a condition. They cannot get work, and consequently pine away for want of nourishment to a degree that if at any time they are accidentally hired to common labor, they have not strength to perform it; and thus the country and themselves are happily delivered from the evils to come.

I have too long digressed, and therefore shall return to my subject. I think the advantages by the proposal which I have made are obvious and many, as well as of the highest importance.

For first, as I have already observed, it would greatly lessen the number of Papists, with whom we are yearly overrun, being the principal breeders of the nation as well as our most dangerous enemies; and who stay at home on purpose to deliver the kingdom to the Pretender, hoping to take their advantage by the absence of so many good Protestants, who have chosen rather to leave their country than to stay at home and pay tithes against their conscience to an Episcopal curate.

Secondly, the poorer tenants will have something valuable of their own, which by law may be made liable to distress, and help to pay their landlord's rent, their corn and cattle being already seized and money a thing unknown.

Thirdly, whereas the maintenance of an hundred thousand children, from two years old and upwards, cannot be computed at less than ten shillings a piece per annum, the nation's stock will be thereby increased fifty thousand pounds per annum, besides the profit of a new dish introduced to the tables of all gentlemen of fortune in the kingdom who have any refinement in taste. And the money will circulate among ourselves, the goods being entirely of our own growth and manufacture.

Fourthly, the constant breeders, besides the gain of eight shillings sterling per annum by the sale of their children, will be rid of the charge of maintaining them after the first year.

Fifthly, this food would likewise bring great custom to taverns, where the vintners will certainly be so prudent as to procure the best receipts for dressing it to perfection, and consequently have their houses frequented by all the fine gentlemen, who justly value themselves upon their knowledge in good eating; and a skillful cook, who understands how to oblige his guests, will contrive to make it as expensive as they please.

Sixthly, this would be a great inducement to marriage, which all wise nations have either encouraged by rewards or enforced by laws and penalties. It would increase the care and tenderness of mothers toward their children, when they were sure of a settlement for life to the poor babes, provided in some sort by the public, to their annual profit instead of expense. We should see an honest emulation among the married women, which of them could bring the fattest child to the market. Men would become as fond of their wives during the time of their pregnancy as they are now of their mares in foal, their cows in calf, or sows when they are ready to farrow; nor offer to beat or kick them (as is too frequent a practice) for fear of a miscarriage.

Many other advantages might be enumerated. For instance, the addition of some thousand carcasses in our exportation of barreled beef, the propagation of swine's flesh, and improvement in the art of making good bacon, so much wanted among us by the great destruction of pigs, too frequent at our tables, which are no way comparable in taste or magnificence to a well-grown, fat yearling child, which roasted whole will make a considerable figure at a lord mayor's feast or any other public entertainment. But this and many others I omit, being studious of brevity.

Supposing that one thousand families in this city would be constant customers for infants' flesh, besides others who might have it at merry meetings, particularly weddings and christenings, compute that Dublin would take off annually about twenty thousand carcasses, and the rest of the kingdom (where probably they will be sold somewhat cheaper) the remaining eighty thousand.

I can think of no one objection that will possibly be raised against this proposal, unless it should be urged that the number of people will be thereby much lessened in the kingdom. This I freely own, and it was indeed one principal design in offering it to this world. I desire the reader will observe, that I calculate my remedy for this one individual kingdom of Ireland and for no other that ever was, is, or I think ever can be upon earth. Therefore let no man talk to me of other expedients: of taxing our absentees at five shillings a pound: of using neither clothes nor household furniture except what is of our own growth and manufacture: of utterly rejecting the materials and instruments that promote foreign luxury: of curing the expensiveness of pride, vanity, idleness, and gaming in our women: of introducing a vein of parsimony, prudence, and temperance: of learning to love our country, in the want of which we differ even from Laplanders and the inhabitants of Topinamboo: of quitting our animosities and factions, nor acting any longer like the Jews, who were murdering one another at the very moment their city was taken: of being a little cautious not to sell our country and conscience for nothing: of teaching landlords to have at least one degree of mercy toward their tenants: lastly, of putting a spirit of honesty, industry, and skill into our shopkeepers; who, if a resolution could be now taken to buy only our native goods, would immediately unite to cheat and exact upon us in the price, the measure and the goodness, nor could ever yet be brought to make one fair proposal of just dealing, though often and earnestly invited to it.

Therefore I repeat, let no man talk to me of these and the like expedients, till he hath at least some glimpse of hope that there will ever be some hearty and sincere attempt to put them in practice.

But as to myself, having been wearied out for many years with offering vain, idle, visionary thoughts, and at length utterly despairing of success, I fortunately fell upon this proposal, which, as it is wholly new, so it hath something solid and real, of no expense and little trouble, full in our own power, and whereby we can incur no danger in disobliging England. For this kind of commodity will not bear exportation, the flesh being of too tender a consistence to admit a long continuance in salt, although perhaps I could name a country which would be glad to eat up our whole nation without it.

After all, I am not so violently bent upon my own opinion as to reject any offer proposed by wise men, which shall be found equally innocent, cheap, easy, and effectual. But before something of that kind shall be advanced in contradiction to my scheme, and offering a better, I desire the author or authors will be pleased maturely to consider two points. First, as things now stand, how they will be able to find food and raiment for an hundred thousand useless mouths and backs. And secondly, there being a round million of creatures in human figure throughout this kingdom, whose sole subsistence put into a common stock would leave them in debt two millions of pounds sterling, adding those who are beggars by profession to the bulk of farmers, cottagers, and laborers, with their wives and children who are beggars in effect; I desire those politicians who dislike my overture, and may perhaps be so bold to attempt an answer, that they will first ask the parents of these mortals whether they would not at this day think it a great happiness to have been sold for food at a year old in the manner I prescribe, and thereby have avoided such a perpetual scene of misfortunes as they have since gone through by the oppression of landlords, the impossibility of paying rent without money or trade, the want of common sustenance, with neither house nor clothes to cover them from the inclemencies of the weather, and the most inevitable prospect of entailing the like or greater miseries upon their breed forever.

I profess, in the sincerity of my heart, that I have not the least personal interest in endeavoring to promote this necessary work, having no other motive than the public good of my country, by advancing our trade, providing for infants, relieving the poor, and giving some pleasure to the rich. I have no children by which I can propose to get a single penny; the youngest being nine years old, and my wife past childbearing.

Discussion Questions

1. Explain Swift's style in terms of sentence lengths, word choice, and attitude.
2. How do Swift's style and tone affect how we read and accept his proposal?

Writing Reflection: Look at one of your arguments written for an earlier assignment. Rewrite it on your own "Modest Proposal."

Grammar Interlude 7: Comma Splice, Semicolon, and Colon

The next three punctuation concerns depend on your understanding of the independent clause to get them right: Comma splices: the cases of the semicolon and the colon.

THE COMMA SPLICE

Comma splices occur because the writer has used only a comma to fuse two Independent clauses together. This is the error. To correct this, the writer needs to place a coordinating conjunction after the comma. Another error writers make to cause comma splices is the use of "however," "therefore," or "nevertheless" as coordinating conjunctions. They are not coordinating conjunctions.

An easy way to remember the coordinating conjunctions is through the acrostic FANBOYS:

For
And
Nor   One of these could solve the comma splice crises.
But
Or
Yet
So

Here's the comma splice:

Jonathan sold many dishwashers that year, he still went broke.

The comma splice is similar to the run-on, except that the writer senses some need to mark off the independent units with a comma.

Here's the correct version:

Jonathan sold many dishwashers that year, but he still went broke.

(Note: If you thought that other ways to correct this error include putting a period or a semicolon after year, you would be correct. A comma splice, which splices complete sentences together, can be solved by separating them. The semicolon acts like the period).

BONUS PUNCTUATION MARKS

These are yours because you have learned the background on them. Take them, use them, and prosper.

Two Punctuation Marks that Require Knowledge of the Independent Clause

Semi Colon   ;   **It's used the same way a period is. But it's used when the two independent clauses you wish to join are closely related in some way.**

Colon   :   **It's used to set up long lists or explanations. But the clause before the colon must always be independent. The common error today with the colon is to have an incomplete sentence before it, as in**

The reasons for the drought are: (Error)

The reasons for the drought include the following: (Correct)

Appendix

Title Writing Workshops

Surprisingly close to the issue of thesis statements are titles. It is not clear that many writers think about them or think about them at the right time in the writing of an essay. But considering a title at a certain point in the process of drafting a paper can help generate ideas and lead to a narrowed focus.

In a finished essay, a title underscores the main idea of a work. In a title, a certain slant, tone, or voice can also appear that should be taken into account when reading the work. When I read—and this is especially true for poetry or short stories—the title guides my understanding. As the first convention encountered, the title is also often the last part of a work to be arrived at. According to many writers, the title comes after an arduous, recursive, communal, and reflective process sustained over many drafts over a length of time. Some published writers acknowledge that they have started a project with a working title, only to see it change as their understanding of their work changed in the process of their writing. *Among the Ash Heaps and Millionaires* was Fitzgerald's working title for *The Great Gatsby* (Bruccoli 207). It is certainly telling in this regard, as is *The Inside of His Head*, Arthur Miller's working title that was later changed to *Death of a Salesman* (Miller 155).

Granted, many titles are written last or even negotiated with an editor. But even if the editor finally supplies the title, of real interest is that the writer not only had a working title, but also that this working title helped the writer through the rewriting of the piece. If the final title becomes part of the organic structure of the work, a thoughtful way into a main concern uniting several threads of thought, the working title gives us keys into understanding something about how the writer envisioned the piece in the early going.

When a writer is guided to engage in rethinking or inventing a title after having generated a rough draft of an assignment, she looks back through what she has written. This becomes an issue not just with creating a title but also of reflecting on how an essay might be revised. Looking again at a title can return a writer to the problem of giving writing a focus.

Four Categories

Consider the following four categories of titles, two of which are poor and two good. The poor categories include one-word titles and those that echo Hamlet's "To Be or Not to Be" dilemma. The good categories include prosaic but competent titles and those that use literary or cultural allusions. It should be clear that these categories are not also the categories for certain levels of a final grade. Rather, the perfectly competent but matter of fact title is effective if the essay follows the title well.

Concerning poor titles, notice the lack of focus they give for the essay. "Gun Control Essay" is the primary example of this, or simply "Gun Control." The second is a variation of the first; both signal that the writer hasn't thought about a focus yet, or that she is trying to include too much in the essay. Indeed, almost without exception, it has been my experience that when I read that title, the essay that follows it will be unfocused, invariably right down to the writer's refusal to settle on a position. Nine out of ten times, as the cliché goes, I can read these titles and know exactly what to say to the writer when we meet in conference to discuss this essay.

The second subsection of the "poor" category is the clichéd title that results from an indulgence in the pseudo-literary, always exemplified by some version of Hamlet's famous "To be or not to be" soliloquy. In a class of twenty students, I will sometimes see as many as eight of these turned in for a given assignment, and "To Control Guns, Or Not," "To Teach or Not to Teach," "To Go to War, or Not To" are all titles I've been handed. As with the one-word titles, the problem is that none of them announces a clear slant. A further problem is the attempt to use literary allusion but to give a cliché instead. The allusion here to Hamlet is the problematic example. As a practice, the use of allusions is literary and usually a piece of snobbery, meant for the insiders—that is, those who have actually read and know the background to the allusion. Hamlet's speech is as universally known as the Old Testament "eye for an eye." Using it defeats the real underlying purpose for using literary allusion, and it also, as a cliché, is too easy.

Effective Titles

Instead of Shakespeare, look for titles not only in literature but also in other areas, perhaps, for example, in popular culture. Real life examples of titles that perform some sort of allusion, literary or cultural, include Woody Allen's *Without Feathers* (taken from a line in an Emily Dickenson poem), Steinbeck's *The Grapes of Wrath* (drawn from a hymn) and *In Dubious Battle* (taken from a line in *Paradise Lost*), O'Connor's "A Good Man Is Hard to Find" (from a popular 1920s song), Hemingway's *For Whom the Bell Tolls* (from John Donne's sermon) and *The Sun Also Rises* (from the Bible), Nathaniel West's *The Day of the Locusts* (also the Bible), and *The Catcher in the Rye* (drawn from a song).

In each of these cases, knowledge of the source from which the title is drawn clarifies and deepens the tone of the work in which the allusion appears. The reader either knows it and is on the inside or seeks to know more about it and is able to bring the context of the allusion to bear on the work in question. And in each case, the context of the secondary passage will either point directly to the main issue to be worked out, deepen irony, or enrich tone, or, in "the best of all possible worlds," accomplish all three.

The Hamlet dlemma mentioned previously, though it may truly underscore a writer's ambivalence about an issue, really does none of this. It's a cliché, used without any thought for the context of the original passage. But there is another problem to using "To be or not to be," and that is the either-or, dualistic terms that must result. Most issues, like those listed above—gun control, effective teaching, and pacifism—are not simple matters of dualism, no matter how often television broadcasts make them seem so.

Focusing briefly on the Hamlet allusion can be an opportunity to consider other less tangible aspects involved in writing. These include not only understanding how literary allusions function, but also the value to writing of reading widely and the problem with using clichés in titles, in images, in the essay itself, and in thinking. Consider that a lack of exposure to literature is not a deficit here. Being a discerning moviegoer can mean an impressive backlog of movie titles available for allusions.

In addition to doing the literary allusion well, or using a popular culture image instead of the cliché, consider also the second "good" category, the competent, matter-of-fact title. This represents the sort of title that works well. Instead of "Gun Control" or "Gun Control Essay," why not something along the lines of "Why the Brady Bill Does Work"? Though plain (certainly not "literary") this one has a clear focus and also tips off a writer's slant.

What is valuable to consider about a competent, matter-of-fact statement of the main focus at the rough stage of an essay is that it may provide the guidance needed for clear thinking about focus. A straightforward statement, as a working title, might lead to deeper thinking later.

Works Cited

Bruccoli, Matthew J. Notes and Preface. *The Great Gatsby.* By F. Scott Fitzgerald. New York: Scribner, 1995: vii-xvi, 207-215.

Miller, Arthur. Introduction to *Collected Plays: Death of a Salesman: Text and Criticism.* By Arthur Miller. Ed. Gerald Weales. New York: Penguin, 1996: 155-171.